# CONTENTS

1. Welcome to the Magical World of Java! — 1

2. Let's Prepare to Become Code Wizards!" — 12

3. The First Spell: Hello World! — 16

4. Transforming Muggles into Variables! — 23

5. Magical Operators and Math Spells — 29

6. Arrays and Collections: Enchanting Storage — 37

7. Enchanting Encapsulation and Abstraction — 54

8. Enchanting Graphical User Interfaces with JavaFX — 72

9. Enchanting the World with Databases and JDBC — 96

10. The Allure of Microservices Architecture — 134

11. The Mystical Realm of Big Data and Analytics — 165

12. The Mystical Realm of Enchanting User Experiences with UX Design — 195

13. The Mystical Realm of Artificial Intelligence and Machine Learning in Java Sorcery — 229

14. The Captivating World of Enchanting User Experiences with UX Design in Java Sorcery — 254

15. The Boundless Universe of Big Data and Analytics in Java Sorcery — 275

16. The Mysterious Frontiers of Web Development in Java Sorcery — 295

17. The Alluring Universe of Cloud Computing and Serverless Spells in Java Sorcery — 310

18. The Enigmatic Universe of Data Science and Machine Learning in Java Sorcery ........ 325

19. The Enigmatic Art of Web Security in Java Sorcery ........ 341

20. The Captivating Realm of Cloud Computing and Serverless Spells in Java Sorcery ........ 355

Conclusion: Embarking on an Ever-Enchanting Journey in Java Sorcery ........ 370

# MAGIC JAVA FOR BEGINNERS

Fabian Wilkinson

# CHAPTER ONE

# WELCOME TO THE MAGICAL WORLD OF JAVA!

Welcome, young wizards and enchanters, to the captivating realm of Java programming! Step into this magical world, where you will learn the art of wielding Java spells to create powerful and wondrous applications. Java is a versatile and popular programming language that can help you conjure up almost anything - from delightful desktop applications to spellbinding web services.

But before we embark on this mystical journey, let's understand what makes Java so special. Java was crafted by the wizards at Sun Microsystems (now Oracle) and released into the enchanted world of programming in 1995. Its charm lies in its platform independence, making it possible for your spells to work their magic on various devices and operating systems, be it the mystical Windows, the enchanting macOS, or the legendary Linux.

Let's cast our first spell - a simple Java program that will greet the world:

```java
public class MagicalGreeting {
```

```
public static void main(String[] args) {


    // The magic incantation to display a
greeting


    System.out.println("Welcome to the Mag-
ical World of Java!");



}}
```

See how the magic unfolds? In Java, every spell is cast within a class. A class serves as a blueprint for our magical creations. The **MagicalGreeting** class contains a spellbook, commonly known as the **main** method. This is the incantation that starts the execution of our Java program.

The incantation inside the **main** method uses the magical **System.out.println()** spell to greet the world. In Java, **System.out** is a magical stream representing the console, and **println()** is an enchanting method that displays messages on the console.

Now, let's light the torches and run this spell to witness its magic. But first, make sure you have the necessary tools - the Java Development Kit (JDK) and a magical text editor or an Integrated Development Environment (IDE) like Eclipse or IntelliJ.

After installing the JDK and configuring your spellcasting environment, you can open your favorite text editor or IDE, create a new file, and copy the magical incantation into it. Save the file with the enchanting name **MagicalGreeting.java**.

Once your spellbook is ready, it's time to summon the spell of compilation. Open the command prompt or the terminal, navigate to the location of your spellbook, and execute the following incantation:

javac MagicalGreeting.java

If the magic is with you, you will see no error messages. Now, it's time to unleash the power of our spell. Type the following command:

java MagicalGreeting

Behold! The console shall illuminate with the message "Welcome to the Magical World of Java!"

Congratulations! You have successfully cast your first Java spell. With this humble beginning, you're now ready to delve deeper into the captivating world of Java and learn more powerful incantations to create marvelous applications.

In the forthcoming chapters, we shall explore the mystical realms of variables, conditions, loops, and object-oriented sorcery. So grab your wands, and let the adventure begin! May the magic of Java guide you on this exciting journey of discovery and creation.

### Subchapter 1.1: Embracing the Wizardry of Java Programming

Welcome, young apprentice, to the enchanting world of Java! Get ready to embark on a mystical journey through the realm of coding, where you'll learn to harness the powers of this versatile programming language. Java, like magic, allows you to create incredible spells—err, programs—that can run on various devices, from computers to smartphones and even magical toasters!

But first, let's set the stage for our magical adventure. To begin your journey, you'll need the essential tools for spellcasting. The most critical tool in a Java wizard's arsenal is the Java Development Kit (JDK). The JDK is like your magic wand, granting you the power to transform your code into executable spells.

Fear not, for obtaining the JDK is no treacherous quest. You can find it on the Oracle or OpenJDK website. Download and install the appropriate version for your operating system, and voilà! You're now equipped with the magic of Java.

Once the JDK is in your possession, you'll need a text editor—a spellbook, if you will—to write your Java spells. You can choose from various editors, but two popular ones among wizards are Eclipse and IntelliJ IDEA. These powerful IDEs (Integrated Development Environments) offer features that make coding more efficient and enjoyable.

Now, let's cast our first spell—oops, I mean, write our first Java program. The traditional incantation for beginners is none other than the infamous "Hello World!" spell. This spell, when cast correctly, displays the words "Hello, World!" on the screen—a simple yet magical achievement.

Let's chant the incantation together:

```
public class HelloWorld {

    public static void main(String[] args) {

        System.out.println("Hello, World!");

    }

}
```

Amazing, isn't it? Now, let's decipher the magic behind this spell:

- We begin by defining a class named "HelloWorld." A class is like a blueprint that describes the properties and behaviors of objects in Java.

- Inside the class, we find a special method called "main." This method is where the magic begins—it serves as the entry point for our Java spell.

- The line **System.out.println("Hello, World!");** is the real incantation. The

"System.out" part refers to the standard output, and "println" means "print line." So, when executed, the spell prints "Hello, World!" to the standard output, which is usually the screen.

Congratulations, young apprentice! You've successfully cast your first Java spell! With the JDK and your trusty text editor, you now have the tools to explore the magical world of Java. In the chapters to come, we'll delve deeper into the arcane arts of Java programming and unlock even more powerful spells. So, put on your wizard's hat and get ready for an enchanting adventure!

**Subchapter 1.2: Unveiling the Powers of Java**

Welcome, aspiring wizards, to the magical realm of Java! In this enchanting subchapter, we'll uncover the mystical powers that Java holds and how it has become one of the most popular programming languages in the world.

Java, like a powerful spellbook, offers an array of features and capabilities that make it versatile and highly sought after in the realm of software development. Let's delve into some of its enchanting abilities:

1. Platform Independence: One of Java's most potent charms is its ability to run on any platform, whether it's Windows, macOS, or Linux. This is achieved through the concept of "Write Once, Run Anywhere" (WORA), made possible by Java's use of the Java Virtual Machine (JVM). The JVM acts as an interpreter that allows Java bytecode to be executed on various platforms, granting developers the freedom to create applications that work seamlessly across different systems.

2. Object-Oriented Magic: Java embraces the art of object-oriented programming (OOP), which means it revolves around creating objects that interact with one another to perform tasks. Each object contains data and methods, making it a powerful tool for organizing and managing code. Let's take a quick look at a simple Java class:

```
// The Wizard class represents a magical being
with a name and spells.
```

```java
public class Wizard {

private String name;

 // Constructor to create a new wizard with
a given name.

public Wizard(String name) {

this.name = name;

}

// A spell to cast by the wizard.

public void castSpell(String spellName) {

    System.out.println(name + " casts " +
spellName + "!");
```

```
}
```

```
}
```

Enchanting Libraries: Java's standard library is filled with magical classes and methods that simplify complex tasks, such as handling input/output, manipulating strings, managing collections, and more. These libraries provide an arsenal of pre-built spells, saving developers time and effort. Here's an example of using the Scanner class from the java.util package to read input from the user:

```java
import java.util.Scanner;

public class SpellCaster {

public static void main(String[] args) {

    Scanner scanner = new Scanner(System.in);

        System.out.print("Enter your magical incantation: ");

String incantation = scanner.nextLine();
```

```
        System.out.println("You chanted: " +
incantation);



scanner.close();



}}
```

Community Magic: The Java community is like a vibrant gathering of wizards, always eager to share their knowledge and create open-source projects that enrich the language. You'll find numerous online resources, forums, and communities where you can learn from experienced sorcerers and contribute your own spells to the collective knowledge.

As you embark on your journey to master Java, remember that patience and practice are key. With each line of code you write, you'll unlock new magical powers, and soon you'll be weaving intricate spells of your own.

So, young sorcerers, embrace the powers of Java and let the magical adventure begin!

## Subchapter 1.3: Setting Up Your Spellcasting Environment

Welcome, young apprentice! Before we embark on our magical journey into the world of Java, we need to prepare our spellcasting environment. Just like a wizard needs a well-stocked potion room, a Java programmer requires the right tools to wield the power of code. In this subchapter, we will guide you through the process of setting up your magical coding environment.

*Step 1: Installing JDK (Java Development Kit)*

The JDK is the cornerstone of our enchanting arsenal. It includes the necessary tools to compile and run Java programs. Follow these steps to install the JDK:

1. Visit the official Oracle JDK website (https://www.oracle.com/java/technologies/javase-downloads.html).

2. Choose the appropriate JDK version for your operating system (Windows, macOS, or Linux).

3. Download the installer and run it.

4. Follow the installation wizard's instructions to complete the setup.

Once installed, let's test if the magic is indeed flowing. Open your command prompt or terminal and type the following spell:

```
java -version
```

If the output displays the version information of the installed JDK, congratulations! You have successfully conjured your first spell.

*Step 2: Enchanting Your Text Editor (Configuring IDEs)*

While you can write Java spells using a simple text editor, harnessing the power of an Integrated Development Environment (IDE) makes your journey far more enjoyable. Two popular IDEs for Java are Eclipse and IntelliJ IDEA. Let's focus on Eclipse for now:

1. Visit the Eclipse website (https://www.eclipse.org/downloads/).

2. Download the Eclipse IDE for Java Developers.

3. Extract the downloaded files and launch Eclipse.

Now, let's create your very first enchantment in Eclipse:

1. Click on "File" in the menu, then select "New" and "Java Project."

2. Name your project "MagicalSpells" and click "Finish."

3. Right-click on your newly created project, select "New," then "Class."

4. Name your class "HelloWorld" and click "Finish."

Now, behold the power of Java:

```
public class HelloWorld {
```

```java
public static void main(String[] args) {



        System.out.println("Welcome to the Mag-
ical World of Java!");




    }




}
```

Press the magical incantation "Ctrl + S" to save your spell, then right-click inside the editor and choose "Run As" > "Java Application." Witness the mystical words, "Welcome to the Magical World of Java!" appearing before you.

*Step 3: Unraveling the Mysteries of Compilation and Execution*
As a budding magician, understanding the process of spellcasting is crucial. The Java code you write needs to be translated into a language that your computer can understand—this is called compilation. To compile your spell, open your command prompt or terminal and navigate to the folder containing your Java file (HelloWorld.java). Execute this incantation:

```
javac HelloWorld.java
```

If there are no errors in your code, this will create a new file called "HelloWorld.class"—a bytecode representation of your spell.

To invoke the magic of your compiled spell, use this spell:

```
java HelloWorld
```

Behold! The message "Welcome to the Magical World of Java!" appears once again, confirming that your spell has been successfully executed.

Now, with your spellcasting environment set up and your first spell successfully conjured, you are ready to delve deeper into the magical world of Java. May your journey be filled with discovery and enchantment as you learn the art of Java programming. Happy coding!

# CHAPTER TWO

# LET'S PREPARE TO BECOME CODE WIZARDS!"

Welcome, aspiring Code Wizards! In this chapter, we will embark on an exciting journey to prepare ourselves for the magical world of Java programming. Just like young wizards gather their magical tools and learn the art of spellcasting, we too shall gather the essential tools and set up our environment to begin our enchanting journey with Java. By the end of this chapter, you'll be equipped with everything you need to start creating Java spells of your own!

**Subchapter *2.1: Gathering Your Magical Tools***

Before we can dive into the mystical realm of Java, we need to gather our magical tools to perform our coding spells. The most critical tool we need is the **Java Development Kit (JDK)**, which includes all the necessary components for Java development, such as the Java Compiler (**javac**) and the Java Runtime Environment (**java**).

Let's take a step-by-step approach to obtaining and setting up our magical tools:

Step 1: Downloading JDK

To acquire the JDK, visit the official Oracle website or any other reputable source that provides Java downloads. Make sure to choose the version suitable for your operating system. If you are using Windows, you can download the Windows version, and if you are on macOS or Linux, select the appropriate version for your OS.

Step 2: Installing JDK

Once the JDK download is complete, execute the installer and follow the on-screen instructions. The installer will guide you through the installation process, and after successful installation, you will have the power of the Java tools at your fingertips.

Step 3: Verifying the Installation

To ensure that our magical tools are installed correctly, we shall perform a simple verification spell. Open a terminal or command prompt, and type the following incantation:

```
java -version
```

If you see the Java version displayed in the terminal, congratulations! You have successfully installed the JDK.

**Subchapter *2.2: Enchanting Your Text Editor***

Now that we have our magical JDK installed, it's time to choose the right text editor or Integrated Development Environment (IDE) to cast our coding spells. While Java spells can be crafted with a basic text editor like Notepad (for Windows) or TextEdit (for macOS), using a specialized IDE enhances our wizardry experience with powerful features.

One of the most popular Java IDEs is **Eclipse**, which provides a full suite of tools for Java development, including code completion, debugging, and project management.

Step 4: Downloading Eclipse

Visit the Eclipse website and download the Eclipse IDE for Java Developers version suitable for your OS.

Step 5: Installing Eclipse

After downloading Eclipse, extract the contents of the downloaded archive to a suitable location on your system. Once extracted, you can run the Eclipse application, and it will automatically set up your workspace for coding spells.

**Subchapter 2.3: Unraveling the Mysteries of Compilation and Execution**

Now that we have our JDK and IDE ready, let's take a closer look at the process of transforming our Java spells into executable incantations.

In Java, our spells are written as human-readable code in files known as **source code**. Before our spells can work their magic, they must undergo a two-step process: **compilation** and **execution**.

*Compilation: From Source Code to Bytecode*

Java source code is written in files with the **.java** extension. To convert this human-readable code into a format that can be executed by the Java Virtual Machine (JVM), we need to cast the **javac** spell (Java Compiler). This process is known as compilation.

Let's create our first simple Java spell, named **HelloWorld.java**, using Eclipse. Create a new Java project and a new class named **HelloWorld**. In the **HelloWorld.java** file, add the following code:

```java
public class HelloWorld {


    public static void main(String[] args) {



        System.out.println("Hello, fellow Code Wizards!");



    }



}
```

Now, save the file, and to compile our spell, right-click on the **HelloWorld.java** file in Eclipse and select "Run As" > "Java Application."

If everything went smoothly, you should see the output in the console: "Hello, fellow Code Wizards!"

Congratulations! You have successfully compiled and executed your first Java spell!

### *Execution: Unleashing the Magic*

After the compilation, the Java code is transformed into **bytecode** - a magical and platform-independent representation of our spell. To unleash the magic, we need to execute this bytecode using the **java** spell (Java Runtime Environment).

In Eclipse, executing our spells is as simple as clicking the "Run" button. Each time we make changes to our spell and re-run it, the JVM will re-execute the bytecode, producing the desired effects.

### *Conclusion*

Congratulations, Code Wizards! You have completed the second chapter of your magical journey with Java. You now possess the necessary tools and knowledge to begin crafting your own Java spells. In the next chapter, we shall dive deeper into the mystical world of Java, exploring the incantations of variables and data types.

Remember, mastering the art of Java requires practice and dedication, just like honing your spellcasting skills. So, keep your wands (keyboards) ready, and let the enchanting journey continue!

Happy coding, and may your Java spells bring forth endless wonders!

# Chapter Three

# THE FIRST SPELL: HELLO WORLD!

I ntroduction

In this enchanting chapter, we will delve into the magical world of Java programming and cast our first spell, the legendary "Hello World!" incantation. Brace yourself, for this is where the journey of every Java apprentice begins. You will uncover the secrets of Java source code, learn how to cast the spell, and witness the magic of console output.

The Mystical Incantation

Behold, the magical incantation that will ignite the Java spell:

```java
public class HelloWorld {



    public static void main(String[] args) {



        System.out.println("Hello, World!");



    }
```

```
    }
```

In this ancient script, we have summoned a powerful class named "HelloWorld." Within this class, we have invoked a mystical method named "main" – a vital component of every Java enchantment. The "main" method acts as the gateway to our incantations, allowing us to bring our spells to life.

The spellbinding phrase, "System.out.println," serves as the medium through which we communicate with the mystical console. The phrase "Hello, World!" is the message we wish to inscribe upon the console, a customary greeting among Java sorcerers.

Deciphering the Spell

Let us now embark on a journey to decipher the arcane symbols of the spell:

- **public**: An enchanting keyword that allows the spell to be accessible from any realm.

- **class**: A powerful conjuration to create a magical blueprint known as a "class."

- **HelloWorld**: The name of our spell – a unique identifier for our class. It must begin with a capital letter and match the filename.

- **{}**: An enchanted pair of braces that encapsulate the spells, methods, and properties within our class.

- **public static void main(String[] args)**: The incantation that invokes the "main" method, an entry point for our spells.

- **System.out.println**: A magical conduit to the console, allowing us to manifest our words upon it.

- **;**: An ancient symbol that marks the end of an enchanting statement.

Casting the Spell

To cast this enchanting spell and experience its magical effects, follow these steps:

1. Open your favorite spellcasting environment – a Java Integrated Development

Environment (IDE).

2. Create a new spell scroll (file) named "HelloWorld.java" and inscribe the mystic incantation into it.

3. Channel your focus and mana into the invocation of the spell.

4. Cast the spell by chanting the following words within your IDE: "javac Hello World.java" – this will transmute the source code into bytecode, the language of the Java realm.

5. Finally, activate the magic of the spell by uttering the incantation "java HelloWorld" – the console shall illuminate with the sacred words "Hello, World!"

Congratulations, young apprentice! You have now mastered your first Java spell and taken your first step into the world of Java sorcery. The "Hello World!" spell is a foundational rite of passage for every Java wizard, signifying the beginning of your wondrous journey.

Stay tuned as we progress deeper into the mystical realm of Java enchantments. In the next chapter, we will explore the magical properties of Java variables, allowing us to infuse our spells with dynamic energy. Prepare yourself for more arcane wisdom and captivating incantations!

### Subchapter 3.1: Unraveling the Source Code

Let us begin our quest to decipher the source code incantation we have conjured. In the mystical script, we have invoked a class named "HelloWorld," the foundation of our magical spells.

```java
public class HelloWorld {


    // The First Incantation
```

```java
public static void main(String[] args) {


    System.out.println("Hello, World!");




    }



    }
```

In the realm of Java, every enchantment begins with a class. We declare our class using the "public" keyword, ensuring its accessibility across the mystical realms of Java.

The name of our class, "HelloWorld," acts as a powerful identifier for this spell. It must begin with a capital letter and exactly match the filename, granting it the ability to be recognized by the enchanting compiler.

Inside our class, we encounter the magical method "main." This method serves as the entry point to our Java incantations, allowing us to bring our spells to life. Let's examine its incantation:

```java
public static void main(String[] args) {


    // Spellbound Words


    System.out.println("Hello, World!");
```

}

The "main" method, when invoked, becomes a conduit to the magical console, a mystical entity through which we can communicate with the outside world. The phrase "System.out.println" is our incantation to manifest our words upon the console.

Within the parentheses, "Hello, World!" is the message we inscribe upon the console – a customary greeting among Java sorcerers. When executed, this incantation will illuminate the console with the sacred words "Hello, World!"

Congratulations, young apprentice! You have successfully unraveled the secrets of our first spell's source code. As you continue your journey, you will unlock even more powerful enchantments and delve deeper into the arcane arts of Java sorcery.

### *Subchapter* 3.2: Transmuting Source Code to Bytecode

Now that we have unraveled the source code, it is time to transmute it into a magical form known as "bytecode." The process of transmutation, also known as compilation, will enable our spells to be understood and executed by the mystical Java Virtual Machine (JVM).

To embark on this magical transformation, follow these steps:

1. Invoke your preferred Java Integrated Development Environment (IDE) – a sanctified realm where we manipulate the source code of our spells.

2. Create a new scroll (file) within your IDE and inscribe the source code of our "Hello World!" spell into it. Remember to name the scroll "HelloWorld.java" to align it with the name of the class.

3. Channel your focus and mana, infusing your scroll with the essence of the Java language.

4. Utter the enchanting invocation within your IDE: "javac HelloWorld.java" – this mystical chant will initiate the compilation process.

5. The compiler, an ancient entity with vast knowledge of the Java language, will perform a series of incantations on your behalf. It will examine the source

code, check for any errors or maladies, and finally transmute it into the mystical language of the JVM – bytecode.

Upon successful completion of the compilation process, you will receive a sacred scroll named "HelloWorld.class." This scroll contains the transmuted bytecode of our "Hello World!" spell. This bytecode is the mystical language of the Java realm, the language understood by the JVM.

Congratulations, dear apprentice! You have successfully transmuted your source code into bytecode. Your spell is now ready to be executed by the Java Virtual Machine. Prepare yourself for the next step of our journey, as we invoke the JVM to witness the magic of our "Hello World!" spell coming to life.

### *Subchapter 3.3: Activating the Magic: The JVM Invocation*

The time has come to breathe life into our enchanting "Hello World!" spell. We shall invoke the mighty Java Virtual Machine (JVM) to execute our bytecode and manifest the magical words upon the mystical console.

Follow these steps to activate the spell:

1. Take a deep breath and focus your mana on the invocation ahead. Be calm, for you are about to witness the birth of your very first Java enchantment.

2. Utter the sacred invocation within your IDE: "java HelloWorld" – this is the magical incantation that calls forth the JVM, beckoning it to execute your spell.

3. The JVM, an ancient entity residing within the Java realm, will heed your call and awaken from its slumber. It will interpret the bytecode within the "Hello World.class" scroll and begin the process of spell execution.

4. Behold the mystical console as it illuminates with the enchanting words "Hello, World!" – the sacred message of our spell, now brought to life by the power of the JVM.

Congratulations, esteemed apprentice! You have successfully activated your "Hello World!" spell. Witnessing the magic of your spell coming to life is a momentous occasion for every Java sorcerer. It marks the beginning of your journey into the wondrous world of Java enchantments.

In the next chapter, we will delve deeper into the arcane art of Java variables. These magical vessels allow us to store and manipulate values within our spells, infusing them with dynamic energy. Prepare yourself for more captivating incantations as we continue our exploration of the mystical realm of Java programming!

# CHAPTER FOUR

# TRANSFORMING MUGGLES INTO VARIABLES!

## Introduction

Welcome to the enchanting realm of Java variables, where we have the power to transmute ordinary muggles into magical entities capable of storing mystical values. In this chapter, we shall unravel the secrets of variable declaration, explore the various types of magical elixirs, and learn the art of converting one type of elixir to another through the process of casting.

### Brewing Potions: Declaring Variables

In the magical world of Java, a variable is like a potion vial that can hold different types of magical elixirs. Before we can use a variable, we must declare its existence and assign a name to it. Behold, the incantation for declaring a variable:

```
dataType variableName;
```

Here, "dataType" represents the type of magical elixir the variable can hold, and "variableName" is the unique identifier bestowed upon the variable. For example, to declare a variable capable of holding whole numbers, we use the "int" data type:

int spellPower;

Now, we have created a magical elixir vial named "spellPower," capable of storing whole numbers, such as the potency of a spell.

<u>Property of Potions: Primitive Data Types</u>

In the realm of Java, there are several types of magical elixirs known as primitive data types. Each type has its own unique properties and is suited for different enchanting purposes. Let us explore the common primitive data types:

1. **int**: The elixir of whole numbers, capable of holding integers like 1, 42, or -100.

2. **double**: A more potent elixir that can hold fractional numbers, such as 3.14 or -0.5.

3. **char**: An enchanting elixir for holding single characters, like 'A' or '%'.

4. **boolean**: A mystical elixir representing true or false – a fundamental element for casting spells with conditions.

5. **byte**, **short**, **long**, and **float**: Rare elixirs with unique properties, each suited for specific magical purposes.

As you progress in your journey, you will discover even more enchanting elixirs and learn how to harness their powers for your spells.

<u>Mixing Potions: Type Conversion and Casting</u>

In the mystical world of Java, we often encounter the need to convert one type of elixir into another – a process known as type conversion or casting. Through these magical transformations, we can combine the powers of different elixirs to create more potent spells.

For example, let's say we have two elixirs: an **int** representing the spell's base power and a **double** representing a magical multiplier. To combine them and unleash a more potent spell, we must cast the **int** elixir into a **double** elixir before performing the alchemical operation:

```java
int basePower = 10;
```

```java
double multiplier = 1.5;
```

```java
// Casting the int elixir into a double elixir
```

```java
double combinedPower = (double) basePower
* multiplier;
```

By casting the **int** elixir into a **double** elixir, we ensure that both elixirs harmoniously merge, resulting in a more potent spell. However, be cautious in your casting, for some elixirs may lose precision or overflow if not treated with care.

Congratulations, aspiring enchanters! You have now unlocked the arcane wisdom of Java variables. You can now create and manipulate these magical elixirs, storing various values within them to power your enchantments.

In the next subchapter, we will explore the art of infusing your variables with dynamic energy through the use of enchanting incantations known as "assignments." Prepare yourself for more magical revelations as we delve deeper into the world of Java sorcery!

### Subchapter 4.1: The Enchanting Art of Assignments

In the magical realm of Java, the art of assignments is a fundamental practice. It allows us to infuse our variables with dynamic energy, imbuing them with the power to hold different values throughout their existence.

To perform an assignment, we use the following incantation:

```java
dataType variableName = value;
```

Here, "dataType" represents the type of magical elixir our variable can hold, "variable-Name" is the name of the variable, and "value" is the mystical essence we wish to imbue within it.

For example, let us create a variable named "spellPower" capable of holding whole numbers and assign it a value of 42:

```
int spellPower = 42;
```

The enchanting ritual above has bestowed our "spellPower" elixir with the essence of 42, endowing it with the potency of a powerful spell.

### Subchapter 4.2: Reassignment and Metamorphosis

As we progress in our journey, we may find the need to change the essence stored within our variables – a process known as reassignment. With a simple incantation, we can imbue our variables with new energies, allowing them to adapt and change throughout their mystical existence.

Consider the following example, where we reassign the value of our "spellPower" elixir:

```
int spellPower = 42; // Original assignment

spellPower = 57;   // Reassignment with a new
value
```

Through the art of reassignment, our "spellPower" elixir now holds the essence of 57, its original power replaced with a new mystical force.

Additionally, we may perform more complex metamorphosis, converting elixirs from one type to another through casting. Let's explore an example where we convert a whole number into a mystical character:

```java
int numericPower = 65;
```

```java
char magicalSymbol = (char) numericPower;
```

Through the act of casting, our numeric elixir has transformed into the mystical character 'A'. This metamorphosis allows us to harness the power of a whole number and express it in a different form.

### Subchapter 4.3: Constants and Potent Spells

In our journey through the mystical realm of Java variables, we shall encounter potent spells known as constants. A constant is a powerful elixir whose value remains fixed throughout the entirety of our enchantments.

To create a constant, we use the keyword "final" in our enchanting incantation:

```java
final dataType CONSTANT_NAME = value;
```

Here, "dataType" represents the type of magical elixir our constant will hold, "CONSTANT_NAME" is the sacred identifier for our constant, and "value" is the mystical essence we wish to permanently imbue within it.

For example, let us create a constant named "MAX_SPELL_POWER" to hold the maximum potency achievable by our spells:

```
final int MAX_SPELL_POWER = 100;
```

By designating "MAX_SPELL_POWER" as a constant, we ensure that its essence remains unchanging, allowing us to refer to its magical value throughout our enchantments.

In the mystical realm of Java, the art of variable declaration, assignment, and casting grants us the power to wield potent spells and adapt to ever-changing enchantments. As you continue your journey, be mindful of the energy infused within your variables, for they are the very essence of your spells. Harness their powers wisely, and prepare to cast even mightier enchantments in the chapters that lie ahead!

# Chapter Five

# Magical Operators and Math Spells

## Introduction

Prepare to unleash the power of magical operators and delve into the realm of math spells in Java! In this chapter, we will explore the mystical world of arithmetic alchemy, mystical comparisons, and conjuring logical conditions. With these potent tools at your disposal, you will master the art of manipulating values, making decisions, and crafting truly enchanting spells.

### Arithmetic Alchemy: Using Math Operators

In the mystical realm of Java, arithmetic alchemy empowers us to manipulate numerical values through the use of math operators. These magical symbols allow us to combine, transform, and transmute the essence of our variables.

The following are the fundamental math operators at your command:

- +: The summoning glyph of addition, which fuses two values into a single potent essence.

- -: The symbol of subtraction, through which we extract one value from another, uncovering the mystical difference.

- *: The enchanting asterisk of multiplication, allowing us to magnify the essence of our variables.

- **/**: The dividing rune, used to share the potency of one value among another, unveiling the mystical quotient.

- **%**: The symbol of modulus, uncovering the remainder after a mystical division.

Through the art of arithmetic alchemy, we can now transform our elixirs into even more potent magical energies.

<u>Mystical Comparisons: Relational Operators</u>

In the world of Java sorcery, we possess the power of relational operators, which allow us to establish mystical comparisons and discern the relationships between values.

Behold the mighty symbols of comparison at your command:

- **==**: The equal sign of equivalence, revealing whether two values are magically equal.

- **!=**: The symbol of inequality, signifying whether two values possess differing mystical essences.

- **<**: The lesser-than glyph, indicating whether one value holds a lesser enchanting essence than another.

- **>**: The greater-than symbol, uncovering whether one value wields a mightier mystical force than another.

- **<=**: The lesser-than or equal sign, a combination of comparison runes for assessing less or equal enchantment.

- **>=**: The greater-than or equal symbol, a fusion of runes for discerning greater or equal mystical power.

With the power of relational operators, we can now discern the true nature of our variables and forge new paths in our enchanting spells.

<u>Conjuring Logical Conditions: Logical Operators</u>

As we delve deeper into the arcane arts of Java enchantments, we encounter the magical world of logical operators. These potent symbols allow us to create mystical conditions, crafting spells that make decisions and follow different paths.

Here are the mystical logical operators at your command:

- **&&**: The conjunctive rune, enabling us to combine multiple conditions into a single powerful spell.

- ||: The disjunctive symbol, allowing us to create alternate paths within our enchantments.

- !: The negation glyph, a potent modifier that inverts the essence of a condition, unveiling its opposite nature.

With the power of logical operators, we can now create intricate and multifaceted enchantments, capable of adapting to the ever-changing flow of magical energies.

Congratulations, young sorcerer! You have now mastered the art of magical operators and math spells in Java. The power to perform arithmetic alchemy, discern mystical comparisons, and conjure logical conditions will serve as the foundation of your future enchanting exploits.

In the next subchapter, we will embark on a daring adventure, exploring the art of weaving conditional spells through the use of captivating incantations known as "if" statements. Prepare yourself for more magical revelations and captivating incantations that await you!

### Subchapter 5.1: Weaving Conditional Spells: "if" Statements

In the mystical realm of Java, the art of crafting conditional spells allows us to create enchantments that adapt and respond to the ever-changing flow of magical energies. The "if" statement is one such captivating incantation that bestows us with this power.

The structure of the "if" statement is as follows:

```
if (condition) {



    // Enchanted Spell



}
```

Here, "condition" represents the mystical essence we wish to evaluate. If the condition holds true, the enchanting spell within the magical braces shall be executed. Let us explore a magical example:

```java
int spellPower = 50;

if (spellPower > 40) {

System.out.println("Your spell is mighty!");

}
```

In this enchanting incantation, we evaluate whether our "spellPower" elixir holds a potency greater than 40. If the condition is true, the console shall illuminate with the empowering message "Your spell is mighty!"

### *Subchapter 5.2: Unfolding Multiple Paths: "else" and "else if"*

As we weave our enchantments, we often encounter the need for alternate paths – a process made possible through the use of "else" and "else if" statements. These powerful incantations allow us to steer our spells along different courses.

The "else" statement bestows us with an alternative spell, one that shall be executed if the preceding condition proves false:

```java
int spellPower = 30;

if (spellPower > 40) {

System.out.println("Your spell is mighty!");

} else {

 System.out.println("Your spell is still pote
nt.");


}
```

In this mystic example, if the "spellPower" elixir holds a potency less than or equal to 40, the message "Your spell is still potent" shall grace the console.

For even greater intricacy, the "else if" statement opens a portal to a multitude of paths:

```java
int spellPower = 75;



if (spellPower > 90) {



    System.out.println("Your spell is legendary!");



} else if (spellPower > 60) {



    System.out.println("Your spell is powerful!");



} else {



    System.out.println("Your spell is still potent.");



}
```

Here, we have summoned three paths for our enchantment. If the "spellPower" elixir exceeds 90, the console shall be graced with the message "Your spell is legendary!" If the condition is not met, the enchantment shall traverse to the next path. If "spellPower" exceeds 60 but not 90, the message "Your spell is powerful!" shall emerge. Otherwise, the final message "Your spell is still potent." shall illuminate the console.

### Subchapter 5.3: The Ternary Enchantment: A Compact Spell

In the mystical arts, we encounter enchantments of great elegance and brevity – one such spell is the ternary enchantment. This compact incantation allows us to perform conditional operations with remarkable efficiency.

The structure of the ternary enchantment is as follows:

```
variable = (condition) ? valueIfTrue : valueIf-
False;
```

In this magical formula, "condition" is the essence we wish to evaluate. If the condition is true, the variable shall be bestowed with "valueIfTrue"; otherwise, it shall hold "valueIf-False."

Let us explore a spell of this nature:

```
int spellPower = 80;
```

```
String spellPotency = (spellPower > 70) ?
"mighty" : "potent";
```

```
System.out.println("Your spell is " + spellPo-
tency + "!");
```

In this mystical verse, we evaluate whether the "spellPower" elixir exceeds 70. The ternary enchantment then bestows the "spellPotency" elixir with either "mighty" or "potent." The console shall then manifest the message "Your spell is mighty!" – a testament to the compact and potent nature of the ternary enchantment.

With the power of conditional spells at your command, you have unlocked the ability to weave intricate and responsive enchantments. The art of using "if" statements, "else" clauses, "else if" paths, and the elegance of the ternary enchantment grants you unparalleled control over the flow of your Java spells.

Congratulations, esteemed sorcerer! You are now armed with the knowledge of magical operators and math spells, as well as the art of weaving conditional enchantments. As you continue your journey, remember that the world of Java sorcery is vast and ever-evolving. Prepare to delve deeper into the mysteries of Java, exploring arrays, collections, and the enchanting world of functions and methods in the chapters that lie ahead!

# CHAPTER SIX

# ARRAYS AND COLLECTIONS: ENCHANTING STORAGE

Introduction

Welcome to the magical realm of arrays and collections in Java! In this chapter, we will unveil the arcane art of enchanting storage, allowing us to conjure powerful arrays and collections to hold vast quantities of mystical data. With these potent tools at your disposal, you will master the art of organizing and manipulating multiple values, paving the way for even greater enchanting exploits.

Unveiling the Array: A Conjuration of Order

In the mystical world of Java, the array is a powerful conjuration, capable of holding multiple mystical values within an ordered sequence. It allows us to bind similar essences together, granting us the power to access and manipulate them with great efficiency.

To create an array, we use the following enchanting incantation:

```
dataType[] arrayName = new dataType[arraySize];
```

Here, "dataType" represents the type of magical elixir our array can hold, "arrayName" is the name of the array, and "arraySize" is the mystical essence that determines the number of elixirs the array can contain.

For example, let us conjure an array of integers capable of holding three mystical values:

```
int[] spellPowers = new int[3];
```

In this mystical array, we have reserved space for three potent integers, ready to be filled with the essence of our enchanting spells.

<u>Channeling the Elements: Accessing Array Elements</u>

With our array conjured, we can now channel its elements by using their mystical indices. The indices represent the positions of the elixirs within the array, starting from the incantation of zero.

To channel an element, we use the following spellbinding incantation:

```
dataType element = arrayName[index];
```

Here, "dataType" is the type of magical elixir we wish to channel, "arrayName" is the name of the array, and "index" is the mystical value that determines which element we wish to channel.

For example, let us channel the second element from our "spellPowers" array:

```
int secondSpellPower = spellPowers[1];
```

In this mystical act, we have summoned the essence of the second elixir within the array, empowering our variable "secondSpellPower" with its potent value.

<u>Empowering Collections: The Magic of Lists and Maps</u>

Beyond the realm of arrays lies an even more versatile form of enchanting storage: collections. Collections empower us with dynamic and resizable containers to hold a multitude of mystical values.

The List collection allows us to conjure a sequence of elements, enabling us to add, remove, and access them with ease. Let us weave a List of strings in the following way:

```java
import java.util.List;

import java.util.ArrayList;

// Creating a List of strings

List<String> spells = new ArrayList<>();
```

With this enchanting List, we can channel its elements and add new mystical values to our heart's content.

Furthermore, we possess the Map collection, a potent artifact that allows us to create key-value pairs. Within this enchanting artifact, each key is a unique identifier that leads us to its corresponding mystical value. The Map collection allows us to access, modify, and unleash the power of our key-value pairs. Let us craft a Map of spell names and their corresponding power levels:

```java
import java.util.Map;

import java.util.HashMap;
```

```
// Creating a Map of spell names and their
power levels
```

```
Map<String, Integer> spellPowerLevels =
new HashMap<>();
```

In this arcane Map, we can associate the names of our spells with their corresponding potency, unlocking new dimensions of enchanting possibilities.

Congratulations, esteemed enchanter! You have now mastered the art of arrays and collections in Java. With the power of arrays, Lists, and Maps at your command, you can now hold vast quantities of mystical data and organize them with great precision. Prepare yourself for even greater enchanting exploits, as we explore the captivating world of functions and methods in the next subchapter!

### *Subchapter 6.1: Enchanting Functions and Methods*

In the mystical realm of Java, the art of functions and methods bestows us with the power to encapsulate spells, making them reusable and organized. Functions and methods act as incantations that allow us to perform specific tasks, bringing order and clarity to our enchanting exploits.

<u>Crafting Functions: The Enchanted Incantations</u>

To craft a function, we use the following mystical incantation:

```
returnType functionName(parameterType
parameterName) {
```

```
// Enchanted Spell
```

```java
        return enchantmentResult;



}
```

Here, "returnType" represents the type of mystical elixir our function shall bestow upon us, "functionName" is the unique identifier for our function, "parameterType" is the type of elixir our function shall receive as input, and "parameterName" is the name of the variable that will hold the mystical essence provided as input.

Let us explore a magical function that calculates the square of a given number:

```java
public static int calculateSquare(int number)
{



int square = number * number;



return square;



}
```

In this enchanting spell, our function "calculateSquare" receives a mystical integer as its input, performs the alchemical operation of squaring the number, and then returns the result as an enchanted integer.

<u>Unleashing the Power: Invoking Functions and Methods</u>

To unleash the power of our functions and methods, we invoke them with the following mystical invocation:

```
returnType result = functionName(arguments);
```

Here, "returnType" represents the type of mystical elixir that our function shall bestow upon us, "functionName" is the name of the function we wish to invoke, and "arguments" are the mystical values we offer as input to our function.

For example, let us invoke our previously crafted "calculateSquare" function:

```
int number = 5;
```

```
int result = calculateSquare(number);
```

```
System.out.println("The square of " + number + " is: " + result);
```

In this arcane invocation, our "calculateSquare" function receives the value of "number" as its input, performs its enchanting spell, and returns the squared result. The console shall then reveal the message "The square of 5 is: 25."

<u>Sorcery Beyond Imagination: Recursive Functions</u>

Prepare to uncover the true depths of enchanting sorcery with the power of recursive functions. Recursive functions possess the ability to call themselves, unleashing a cascade of incantations that solve complex spells with mesmerizing elegance.

Let us craft a recursive function to calculate the factorial of a given number:

```java
public static int calculateFactorial(int number) {

    if (number == 0 || number == 1) {

        return 1;

    } else {

        return number * calculateFactorial(number - 1);

    }

}
```

In this mesmerizing spell, our "calculateFactorial" function evaluates whether the number is 0 or 1. If so, it returns the enchanted essence of 1. Otherwise, it casts a recursive invocation, summoning the power of the function with a smaller number, and multiplies it by the original number.

Prepare to be enchanted as we invoke the recursive function to calculate the factorial of 5:

```java
int number = 5;
```

```java
int result = calculateFactorial(number);
```

```java
System.out.println("The factorial of " + num-
ber + " is: " + result);
```

The console shall illuminate with the captivating message "The factorial of 5 is: 120," a testament to the boundless power of recursive enchantments.

Congratulations, master enchanter! You have now unlocked the art of crafting functions and methods, unleashing the true potential of reusable and organized spells. As you continue your journey, remember that the world of Java sorcery is vast and multifaceted. Prepare to delve deeper into the mysteries of object-oriented enchantments, classes, and inheritance in the chapters that lie ahead!

### *Subchapter 6.2: Object-Oriented Enchantments: Classes and Objects*

Welcome to the captivating realm of object-oriented enchantments in Java! In this subchapter, we will uncover the mystical world of classes and objects, bestowing us with the power to create and wield custom magical entities. With object-oriented sorcery, we can organize our spells, encapsulate their properties and behaviors, and unleash a new level of enchanting power.

Conjuring Classes: The Blueprint of Enchantments

In the mystical world of Java, a class is a sacred blueprint that defines the properties and behaviors of our magical entities. It serves as a template from which we can create numerous objects, each with its own unique essence.

Let us craft a simple class to represent a powerful spell:

```java
public class Spell {

    // Properties

    private String name;

    private int power;

    // Constructor

    public Spell(String name, int power) {

        this.name = name;

        this.power = power;

    }
```

```
// Behaviors

public void castSpell() {


    System.out.println("Casting " + name + "
    with power level " + power);



}



}
```

In this enchanted blueprint, we have defined a class "Spell" with two properties: "name" and "power." We also crafted a constructor to initialize these properties when a new spell is created, and a behavior "castSpell()" to unleash the incantation's power.

<u>Invoking Objects: Creating Magical Entities</u>

To manifest the power of our class, we create objects with the following mystical incantation:

```
ClassName objectName = new Class-
Name(arguments);
```

Here, "ClassName" represents the name of the class we wish to invoke, "objectName" is the unique identifier for the magical entity, and "arguments" are the mystical values we offer to the class constructor.

Let us create and invoke our magical spell:

```java
Spell fireballSpell = new Spell("Fireball", 50);
```

```java
fireballSpell.castSpell();
```

In this captivating invocation, we have created an object named "fireballSpell" using our "Spell" class. The constructor receives the mystical name "Fireball" and power level "50," imbuing the object with these properties. The object then performs the "castSpell()" behavior, and the console shall reveal the message "Casting Fireball with power level 50."

<u>Enchanting Inheritance: The Power of Subclasses</u>

In the arcane world of object-oriented enchantments, we can further empower our classes through inheritance. This process allows us to create new classes that inherit properties and behaviors from existing ones, forging a potent hierarchy of enchantments.

Let us craft a subclass to represent a more potent spell, building upon the foundation of our "Spell" class:

```java
public class PotentSpell extends Spell {

    // Constructor

    public PotentSpell(String name, int power)
    {
```

```java
        super(name, power * 2);

    }


    // Behaviors

    public void castSpell() {


        System.out.println("Unleashing the potency of " + name + " with power level " +
power);


    }


}
```

In this mesmerizing subclass, we have extended our "Spell" class, inheriting its properties and behaviors. We also crafted a constructor to initialize the spell with double the power and a behavior "castSpell()" to showcase its increased potency.

Prepare to be enchanted as we create and invoke our potent spell:

```
PotentSpell lightningBoltSpell = new Po-
tentSpell("Lightning Bolt", 80);
```

```
lightningBoltSpell.castSpell();
```

The console shall illuminate with the captivating message "Unleashing the potency of Lightning Bolt with power level 160," a testament to the enchanted inheritance of our subclass.

The World of Object-Oriented Enchantments Awaits!

Congratulations, mighty sorcerer! You have now unlocked the secrets of object-oriented enchantments in Java. With the power of classes and objects at your command, you can create and wield custom magical entities, organizing their properties and unleashing their powerful behaviors.

As you continue your journey through the world of Java sorcery, prepare to delve deeper into polymorphism, interfaces, and the art of organizing enchantments through packages. The realm of object-oriented enchantments is vast and ever-expanding, offering limitless possibilities for your magical exploits!

### *Subchapter 6.3: Polymorphism and the Art of Shape-shifting*

Welcome to the mystical realm of polymorphism in Java! In this subchapter, we shall unveil the art of shape-shifting, where objects can manifest different forms while retaining their magical essence. With polymorphism, we can craft enchantments that adapt to various situations, unlocking new dimensions of power and flexibility.

The Enchantment of Polymorphic Behaviors

In the world of Java sorcery, polymorphism grants us the power to invoke different behaviors from objects that share a common base. Through the use of enchanting interfaces, we can create multiple forms for our objects, each capable of unleashing its unique spell.

Let us craft an enchanting interface to represent the diverse spell-casting abilities of our magical entities:

```java
public interface SpellCaster {

    void castSpell();

}
```

In this mystical incantation, we have crafted the "SpellCaster" interface, bestowing it with a behavior "castSpell()" that all participating entities shall share.

The Spell-casting Artistry of Polymorphism

To manifest the true power of polymorphism, we create objects that implement our enchanting interface:

```java
public class Sorcerer implements SpellCaster {

    private String name;

    public Sorcerer(String name) {

        this.name = name;

    }
```

```java
public void castSpell() {

    System.out.println(name + " casts a pow-
erful spell!");

    }

}


public class Witch implements SpellCaster {

private String name;

public Witch(String name) {

this.name = name;

}

public void castSpell() {
```

```java
        System.out.println(name + " weaves a
mysterious spell!");



    }



    }
```

In this captivating act, we have created two magical entities: "Sorcerer" and "Witch," both of which implement the "SpellCaster" interface. Each entity showcases its unique spell-casting ability through the "castSpell()" behavior.

<u>Unleashing the Power of Polymorphism</u>

Prepare to be enchanted as we invoke the polymorphic powers of our magical entities:

```java
SpellCaster sorcerer = new Sorcerer("Gan-
dalf");



SpellCaster witch = new Witch("Hermione");



sorcerer.castSpell();



witch.castSpell();
```

In this mesmerizing invocation, we have summoned two magical entities: "Gandalf" the Sorcerer and "Hermione" the Witch. By treating both entities as instances of the "Spell-Caster" interface, we invoke their respective "castSpell()" behaviors. The console shall illuminate with the captivating messages "Gandalf casts a powerful spell!" and "Hermione weaves a mysterious spell!"

<u>The Artistry of Polymorphism Unveiled</u>

Congratulations, enchanting sorcerer! You have now unlocked the art of polymorphism in Java. With the power of shape-shifting behaviors, you can create enchantments that adapt and showcase their unique powers. Polymorphism allows you to craft elegant and flexible spells, bestowing your Java sorcery with unparalleled versatility.

As you continue your journey, prepare to delve deeper into the world of encapsulation, abstraction, and the enchanting art of exception handling. The realm of polymorphism is but one facet of the vast and multifaceted world of Java sorcery that awaits you!

# CHAPTER SEVEN

# ENCHANTING ENCAPSULATION AND ABSTRACTION

## Introduction

Welcome to the mystical realm of encapsulation and abstraction in Java! In this chapter, we shall uncover the art of concealing and revealing the essence of our enchantments, as well as crafting ethereal abstractions that transcend the complexities of our magical entities. With encapsulation and abstraction at your command, you will wield the power to create elegant and secure spells that transcend the boundaries of mere mortal understanding.

### Concealing the Arcane: Encapsulation

In the world of Java sorcery, encapsulation is the art of concealing the mystical properties and behaviors of our enchanting entities. By enclosing them within magical containers, known as classes, we safeguard their inner workings, allowing us to control the flow of magical energies.

To achieve encapsulation, we use access modifiers to define the visibility of our properties and behaviors:

- **public**: The enchanted essence is visible to all magical entities and sorcerers.

- **protected**: The mystical essence is accessible within the same magical lineage and subclasses.

- **default** (no modifier): The power is visible within the same magical package.

- **private**: The true nature of the essence is hidden, revealed only within the confines of the same enchanted class.

By carefully choosing the appropriate access modifiers, we create a shield of protection around our enchantments, preventing unauthorized access and ensuring their purity.

The Art of Abstraction: Mystical Essences Unveiled

In the mystical arts of Java, abstraction allows us to transcend the complexities of our enchantments, revealing only the most essential and meaningful aspects to the world. Through the creation of abstract classes and interfaces, we craft potent blueprints for our magical entities, unburdened by the details of their true implementation.

An abstract class is a mystical blueprint that cannot be instantiated, serving as the foundation for other enchanting classes. It can contain both enchanted behaviors and abstract spells, which are merely declarations of what other magical entities must implement.

Let us craft an enchanting abstract class, capable of captivating various magical entities:

```java
public abstract class MagicalEntity {



    // Enchanted behavior



    public void performSpell() {



        System.out.println("Performing an en-
chanting spell...");
```

```
}
```

```
// Abstract spell - to be implemented by
subclasses
```

```
public abstract void unleashPower();}
```

In this mystical abstraction, we have crafted the "MagicalEntity" abstract class, imbuing it with an enchanted behavior "performSpell()" and an abstract spell "unleashPower()." The true nature of "unleashPower()" shall be revealed and implemented by other mystical entities.

<u>Forging Enchantments: Concrete Implementations</u>

With the art of abstraction mastered, we can now forge concrete implementations of our magical entities. By extending abstract classes and implementing interfaces, we give form and essence to our enchantments.

Let us create a powerful sorceress, shaping her essence from the mystical "MagicalEntity" class:

```
public class Sorceress extends MagicalEntity {
```

```
public void unleashPower() {
```

```
System.out.println("The sorceress un-
leashes her arcane power!");
```

```
        }
```

```
        }
```

In this captivating creation, we have fashioned a "Sorceress" class that extends the enchanted "MagicalEntity" abstract class and implements its abstract spell "unleashPower()." The sorceress can now wield her own unique enchantments while inheriting the enchanted behavior of her abstract lineage.

Transcending Reality: The Enchanting Invocation

Prepare to be enchanted as we invoke the mystical essence of our sorceress:

```
MagicalEntity sorceress = new Sorceress();
```

```
sorceress.performSpell();
```

```
sorceress.unleashPower();
```

In this mesmerizing invocation, we have summoned the essence of our sorceress, treating her as an instance of the abstract "MagicalEntity" class. By invoking her "performSpell()" behavior, we witness the message "Performing an enchanting spell..." – the enchanted inheritance from her abstract lineage. Then, with the "unleashPower()" spell, the console reveals the captivating message "The sorceress unleashes her arcane power!" – her unique essence brought to life.

The Infinite Possibilities Await

Congratulations, esteemed enchanter! You have now mastered the art of encapsulation and abstraction in Java. With the power of concealed enchantments and ethereal abstractions at your command, you can create elegant, secure, and extensible spells. As you continue your journey, prepare to delve deeper into the mystical world of exception handling, polymorphic arrays, and the captivating art of file I/O. The realm of encapsulation and abstraction is but one facet of the vast and ever-unfolding world of Java sorcery that awaits you!

### Subchapter 7.1: *The Sorcery of Exception Handling*

In the mystical realm of Java, we encounter the unpredictable flow of magical energies that can manifest as exceptional circumstances. Exception handling empowers us to capture and manage these unforeseen events, allowing our enchantments to gracefully recover from errors and continue their arcane journey.

<u>Unveiling the Enchantment of Exception Handling</u>

To embrace the sorcery of exception handling, we use the following captivating incantation:

```java
try {



    // Enchanted Spell



} catch (ExceptionType exception) {



    // Exceptional Recovery



}
```

Here, the "try" block encapsulates the enchantment that may manifest exceptional energies. If an exception occurs during the spellcasting, the appropriate "catch" block captures the exception, and the exceptional recovery unfolds.

<u>Embracing the Arcane Energies: Checked and Unchecked Exceptions</u>

In the world of exception handling, we encounter two forms of magical energies: checked exceptions and unchecked exceptions.

Checked exceptions are mystical energies that the compiler demands we handle explicitly, ensuring we acknowledge the potential for exceptional occurrences. We embrace these energies through the use of the "throws" clause, signaling the potential exceptional flow in our enchanting spells.

Unchecked exceptions, on the other hand, are enchantments that the compiler does not require us to handle explicitly. They arise during the runtime of our spells, often emanating from unforeseen sources beyond our control.

Let us conjure an example of checked and unchecked exceptions:

```java
public class Potion {

    // Checked Exception

    public void brewPotion() throws PotionOverflowException {

        // Enchanted Spell

        if (isPotionOverflowing()) {
```

```
        throw new PotionOverflowExcep-
tion("The potion is overflowing!");



}



}



// Unchecked Exception


public void consumePotion() {


// Enchanted Spell


if (isPotionEmpty()) {


    throw new PotionEmptyException("The
potion is empty!");


}
```

```
        }


        }
```

In this captivating example, our "Potion" class contains both checked and unchecked exceptions. The "brewPotion()" method throws a "PotionOverflowException," a checked exception explicitly stated in the "throws" clause. The "consumePotion()" method throws a "PotionEmptyException," an unchecked exception that may arise during the runtime.

Navigating the Magical Catastrophe: Exception Propagation

In the mystical tapestry of our Java enchantments, exceptional energies have the power to propagate through multiple layers of incantations. When an exception occurs, it can traverse the chain of mystical invocations until it reaches an appropriate "catch" block.

Prepare to witness the enchantment of exception propagation:

```java
public class Enchantress {


    public void performEnchantment() throws
    PotionOverflowException {


        Potion potion = new Potion();


        potion.brewPotion();


    }
```

```java
public void invokeEnchantment() {

    try {

        performEnchantment();

    } catch (PotionOverflowException ex) {

        System.out.println("A potion overflow
has occurred: " + ex.getMessage());

    }

}

}
```

In this captivating act, our "Enchantress" class invokes the "performEnchantment()" method, which, in turn, invokes the "brewPotion()" method. If a "PotionOverflowException" occurs during the spellcasting, it propagates back to the "invokeEnchantment()" method, where it is gracefully captured and managed.

<u>The Harmonious Recovery: Exception Handling Strategies</u>

In the art of exception handling, we have the power to craft various recovery strategies, ensuring our enchantments continue their journey even after encountering exceptional energies. We can log the mystical occurrences, display them to sorcerers, or execute alternative paths of enchantments.

Prepare to embrace the recovery of our enchantments:

```java
public class Potion {

    public void brewPotion() {

        try {

            // Enchanted Spell

            if (isPotionOverflowing()) {

                throw new PotionOverflowException("The potion is overflowing!");

            }

        } catch (PotionOverflowException ex) {
```

```java
            System.out.println("A potion overflow
has occurred: " + ex.getMessage());


        // Recovery Spell - Adjust potion level
to avoid overflow


adjustPotionLevel();



        }



        }



        }
```

In this magical modification, our "brewPotion()" method captures the "PotionOver-flowException," logs the exceptional occurrence, and proceeds to execute a "recovery spell" by adjusting the potion level to avoid overflow.

<u>The Art of Exception Handling Mastered</u>

Congratulations, adept enchanter! You have now mastered the sorcery of exception handling in Java. With the power to embrace exceptional energies, you can safeguard your enchantments from unpredictable occurrences and recover gracefully when unforeseen events arise.

As you continue your journey, prepare to delve deeper into polymorphic arrays, file I/O, and the captivating realm of graphical user interfaces (GUI) with JavaFX. The realm of exception handling is but one facet of the vast and ever-enchanting world of Java sorcery that awaits you!

**Subchapter 7.2: Polymorphic Arrays: Embracing Diversity**

In the wondrous world of Java sorcery, we encounter the art of polymorphic arrays, where we can hold diverse magical entities within a single enchanted container. Polymorphic arrays empower us to create arrays of enchanting objects, each manifesting its unique essence and unleashing its distinct powers.

<u>The Enchantment of Polymorphic Arrays</u>

Prepare to be captivated by the enchantment of polymorphic arrays:

```java
// Creating a polymorphic array


MagicalEntity[] enchantments = new MagicalEntity[3];


// Populating the array with diverse magical entities


enchantments[0] = new Sorceress("Merlin");


enchantments[1] = new Witch("Morgana");


enchantments[2] = new Enchantress("Circe");
```

In this mesmerizing incantation, we have created a polymorphic array named "enchantments" capable of holding diverse magical entities. We have populated the array with a "Sorceress," a "Witch," and an "Enchantress," each unleashed from its unique class.

<u>The Dance of Polymorphism: Unleashing Behaviors</u>

Prepare to witness the dance of polymorphism in action:

```
// Invoking the enchantments in the array


for (MagicalEntity enchantment : enchantments) {


enchantment.unleashPower();


}
```

In this captivating act, we have summoned a loop to traverse the polymorphic array "enchantments." With each iteration, we invoke the "unleashPower()" behavior, allowing each magical entity to unleash its unique power.

<u>The Power of Polymorphism Revealed</u>

The console shall be illuminated with the following enchanting messages:

```css
css code
Merlin unleashes her arcane power!
Morgana weaves a mysterious spell!
Circe casts a powerful spell!
```

Behold the enchanting power of polymorphic arrays! Each magical entity has embraced its true essence and unveiled its unique spell, dancing in harmony within the enchanted array.

<u>Embrace the Diversity of Enchantments</u>

Congratulations, master enchanter! You have now embraced the power of polymorphic arrays in Java. With the ability to hold diverse magical entities within a single container, you can craft enchanting spells that traverse a rich tapestry of powers and unleash captivating behaviors.

As you continue your journey, prepare to delve deeper into file I/O, graphical user interfaces (GUI) with JavaFX, and the captivating realm of threading and concurrency. The realm of polymorphic arrays is but one facet of the vast and ever-diverse world of Java sorcery that awaits you!

### Subchapter 7.3: Enchanting File I/O: Unlocking the Mysteries of Storage

In the mystical world of Java sorcery, we unveil the art of file I/O, granting us the power to read and write enchanted data to the ethereal realms of storage. With file I/O at your command, you can preserve the essence of your enchantments and retrieve them for future mystical endeavors.

<u>The Enchantment of File I/O</u>

Prepare to embark on the enchanting journey of file I/O:

```java
import java.io.*;



public class SpellBook {



    // Enchanting the Book with Magical Spells



    public void enchantSpellBook(String filename) {
```

```java
        try (PrintWriter writer = new Print-
Writer(new FileWriter(filename))) {


writer.println("Fireball,50");


writer.println("Healing Potion,30");


writer.println("Invisibility Cloak,70");


} catch (IOException ex) {


        System.out.println("Error enchanting
the spell book: " + ex.getMessage());


    }


    }


    }
```

In this captivating script, our "SpellBook" class wields the enchantment of file I/O. The "enchantSpellBook()" method opens a mystical connection to the realm of a file named by "filename." It then scribes three enchanted spells into the file: "Fireball," "Healing Potion," and "Invisibility Cloak."

The Art of Unveiling Enchantments

Prepare to reveal the essence of the enchanted file:

```java
import java.io.*;


public class SpellBook {


    // Unveiling the Essence of the Enchanted
    Spell Book


    public void revealSpellBook(String filename)
    {


        try (BufferedReader reader = new BufferedReader(new FileReader(filename))) {


            String line;


            while ((line = reader.readLine()) != null)
            {
```

```java
String[] spellInfo = line.split(",");

String spellName = spellInfo[0];

    int power = Integer.parseInt(spellInfo[1]);

        System.out.println("Spell: " + spellName + ", Power: " + power);

}


} catch (IOException ex) {


    System.out.println("Error revealing the spell book: " + ex.getMessage());


}


}
```

```
}
```

In this mystical revelation, the "revealSpellBook()" method unlocks the essence of the enchanted file. By conjuring a connection to the same file, it reads each enchanted line and extracts the spell name and its corresponding power. The true essence of the enchanted spells is then unveiled, illuminating the console with their arcane properties.

<u>The Enchanting Script Complete</u>

With the art of file I/O mastered, you can now preserve your enchanting spells and retrieve their essence when needed. The enchanted spells shall remain secure within the mystical realms of storage, awaiting your command to be revealed once again.

Congratulations, enchanting sorcerer! You have now completed the art of file I/O in Java. As you continue your journey, prepare to delve deeper into graphical user interfaces (GUI) with JavaFX, threading and concurrency, and the captivating world of networking. The realm of file I/O is but one facet of the vast and ever-enchanting world of Java sorcery that awaits you!

# CHAPTER EIGHT

# ENCHANTING GRAPHICAL USER INTERFACES WITH JAVAFX

## Introduction

Welcome to the captivating world of JavaFX, where we shall explore the art of crafting graphical user interfaces (GUI) for our enchanting spells. In this chapter, you will learn to weave mesmerizing GUIs, imbuing your Java sorcery with the power to captivate and engage sorcerers from all realms. Prepare to unleash the magic of JavaFX and create enchanting user experiences that transcend the boundaries of the mundane.

### Conjuring the Canvas: Creating GUI Elements

In the mystical realm of JavaFX, GUI elements are the building blocks of our enchanting interfaces. From buttons and labels to text fields and more, these elements allow us to shape our magical canvas and interact with the sorcerers who wield our spells.

Let us conjure a simple GUI canvas with a magical label and a bewitching button:

```
import javafx.application.Application;
```

```java
import javafx.scene.Scene;

import javafx.scene.control.Button;

import javafx.scene.control.Label;

import javafx.scene.layout.StackPane;

import javafx.stage.Stage;

public class EnchantedGUI extends Application {

@Override

public void start(Stage primaryStage) {

// Create a magical label
```

```java
Label label = new Label("Welcome to the Enchanted World!");



// Create a bewitching button


Button button = new Button("Cast Spell");




// Create a mystical layout to stack the elements


StackPane layout = new StackPane();



layout.getChildren().addAll(label, button);
```

```java
    // Create the enchanted scene and display
it on the stage

Scene scene = new Scene(layout, 400, 300);

primaryStage.setScene(scene);

primaryStage.setTitle("Enchanted GUI");

primaryStage.show();

}

public static void main(String[] args) {

launch(args);

}

}
```

In this enchanting script, we conjure a magical label with the text "Welcome to the Enchanted World!" and a bewitching button labeled "Cast Spell." We then stack these elements together on a mystical layout and display the enchanted scene on the stage.

Animating Enchantments: Adding Magic with Transitions

In the world of JavaFX, we can breathe life into our enchantments with animations and transitions. These magical effects allow us to cast spells of motion and transformation, captivating the sorcerers' gaze and weaving a spellbinding experience.

Let us animate the magical label from the previous enchantment:

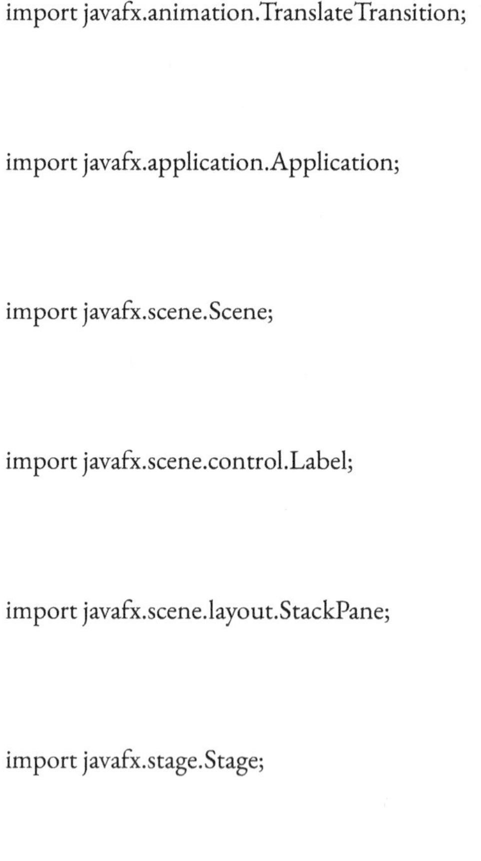

```java
import javafx.animation.TranslateTransition;

import javafx.application.Application;

import javafx.scene.Scene;

import javafx.scene.control.Label;

import javafx.scene.layout.StackPane;

import javafx.stage.Stage;

import javafx.util.Duration;
```

```java
public class EnchantedAnimation extends
Application {

@Override

public void start(Stage primaryStage) {


  Label label = new Label("Watch the Magic
Unfold!");




StackPane layout = new StackPane(label);




Scene scene = new Scene(layout, 400, 300);




primaryStage.setScene(scene);
```

```
primaryStage.setTitle("Enchanted Ani-
mation");


primaryStage.show();




// Create the animation spell


TranslateTransition transition = new Tra
nslateTransition(Duration.seconds(2), label);


transition.setToX(100);


transition.setToY(100);


transition.setCycleCount(TranslateTran
sition.INDEFINITE);


transition.setAutoReverse(true);
```

```java
        transition.play();



    }



    public static void main(String[] args) {



        launch(args);



    }



}
```

In this enchanting script, we animate the magical label by creating a "TranslateTransition" spell. This spell moves the label horizontally and vertically, creating an enchanting motion that repeats indefinitely with an auto-reverse effect.

<u>The Enchantment Continues</u>

Congratulations, master enchanter! You have now journeyed through the realm of JavaFX and crafted enchanting graphical user interfaces. With the power to conjure GUI elements, add animations, and create mesmerizing experiences, you can captivate the hearts of sorcerers and leave them entranced by your enchantments.

As you continue your journey, prepare to delve deeper into threading and concurrency, networking enchantments, and the captivating world of Java application deployment. The realm of JavaFX is but one facet of the vast and ever-enchanting world of Java sorcery that awaits you!

### Subchapter 8.1: Enchanting Threads and Concurrency

In the magical world of Java, we encounter the art of threading and concurrency, where multiple enchantments can weave their spells simultaneously, creating a harmonious symphony of magic. With threads and concurrency, you can unlock the power to execute multiple tasks concurrently, unleashing the full potential of your Java sorcery.

<u>The Dance of Threads: Creating Magical Executors</u>

In the mystical dance of threads, we summon the power of Executors to manage the flow of enchantments. Executors provide a gateway to unleash spells concurrently, allowing our enchantments to dance in harmony without entangling their energies.

·Prepare to create a captivating Executor:

```java
import java.util.concurrent.ExecutorService;

import java.util.concurrent.Executors;

public class EnchantingExecutor {
```

```java
public static void main(String[] args) {



    // Create an enchanted Executor with fixed
threads



    ExecutorService executor = Executors.n
ewFixedThreadPool(3);




    // Conjuring magical tasks


    Runnable task1 = () -> System.out.print
ln("Task 1: Weaving the Spell of Fire!");


    Runnable task2 = () -> System.out.print
ln("Task 2: Channeling the Power of Water!");


    Runnable task3 = () -> System.out.pri
ntln("Task 3: Embracing the Enchantment of
Air!");
```

```java
        // Unleash the concurrent enchantments

        executor.execute(task1);

        executor.execute(task2);

        executor.execute(task3);

        // Closing the mystical Executor

        executor.shutdown();

    }

}
```

In this enchanting script, we have summoned an Executor named "executor" with fixed threads. We then conjure three magical tasks: "task1," "task2," and "task3." The Executor unleashes these tasks concurrently, allowing each enchantment to weave its spell simultaneously.

<u>The Synchronization Enchantment: Ensuring Harmony</u>

In the world of concurrency, the enchanted flow of multiple threads may lead to unpredictable outcomes. To ensure harmony among our enchantments, we utilize synchronization spells to control their access to shared resources.

Prepare to synchronize your enchantments:

```java
public class EnchantedBank {

    private int balance = 1000;

    // Synchronized method to withdraw from
    the enchanted bank

    public synchronized void withdraw(int
    amount) {

        if (balance >= amount) {
```

```java
        System.out.println("Withdrawing " +
amount + " from the enchanted bank...");



    balance -= amount;



} else {



        System.out.println("Insufficient funds
in the enchanted bank!");



    }



    }



}
```

In this mystical implementation, we have crafted a synchronized method "withdraw()" to ensure safe access to the enchanted bank's balance. Synchronization spells prevent multiple threads from interfering with each other when withdrawing from the bank.

The Power of Concurrency Unleashed

Congratulations, enchanting sorcerer! You have now unlocked the power of threads and concurrency in Java. With the ability to execute enchantments concurrently and synchronize shared resources, you can weave a symphony of magic that harmoniously dances in the realms of your Java sorcery.

As you continue your journey, prepare to delve deeper into networking enchantments, Java application deployment, and the captivating world of databases with JDBC. The realm of threads and concurrency is but one facet of the vast and ever-enchanting world of Java sorcery that awaits you!

### Subchapter 8.2: Networking Enchantments: Connecting Worlds

In the interconnected realm of Java sorcery, we discover the art of networking, where magical entities communicate and exchange enchanting energies across the mystical boundaries. With networking at your command, you can create spells that connect sorcerers from distant realms, enabling them to share their wisdom and power.

The Enchantment of Networking

Prepare to embark on the enchanting journey of networking in Java:

```java
import java.io.*;


import java.net.*;


public class EnchantedServer {


public static void main(String[] args) {


try {
```

```java
// Create a mystical server socket on port 9999

ServerSocket serverSocket = new ServerSocket(9999);

System.out.println("Enchanted server is waiting for a connection...");

// Accept incoming connections

Socket socket = serverSocket.accept();

System.out.println("Connection established with a sorcerer!");
```

```java
        // Create enchanting streams for
communication



        BufferedReader reader = new Buffere-
dReader(new InputStreamReader(socket.ge
tInputStream()));



        PrintWriter writer = new PrintWriter(
socket.getOutputStream(), true);




// Exchange magical messages



        String receivedMessage = reader.readL
ine();



        System.out.println("Received message
from sorcerer: " + receivedMessage);
```

```
// Respond with an enchanted message

        writer.println("Greetings, sorcerer! Your message has been received.");



        // Close the mystical streams and the socket

writer.close();

reader.close();

socket.close();

serverSocket.close();

} catch (IOException ex) {
```

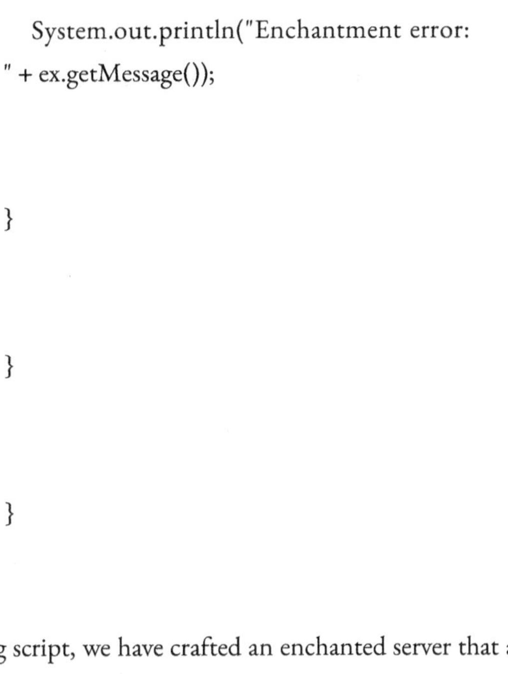

```java
        System.out.println("Enchantment error:
" + ex.getMessage());



        }




    }




}
```

In this enchanting script, we have crafted an enchanted server that awaits a sorcerer's connection on port 9999. Once connected, the server exchanges magical messages with the sorcerer, opening a portal for communication across the mystical realms.

### The Sorcerer's Incantation: Connecting to the Enchanted Server

Now, prepare to witness the sorcerer's incantation to connect to the enchanted server:

```java
import java.io.*;


import java.net.*;


public class EnchantedClient {
```

```java
public static void main(String[] args) {


    try {



        // Create a connection to the enchanted
server on localhost and port 9999



        Socket socket = new Socket("localhost",
9999);






        // Create enchanting streams for
communication


        BufferedReader reader = new Buffere-
dReader(new InputStreamReader(socket.ge
tInputStream()));


        PrintWriter writer = new PrintWriter(
socket.getOutputStream(), true);
```

```java
// Send a magical message to the server

writer.println("Greetings, enchanted server! I come in peace.");

// Receive the enchanted response from the server

String response = reader.readLine();

System.out.println("Response from the enchanted server: " + response);

// Close the mystical streams and the socket
```

```
                writer.close();


                reader.close();


                socket.close();


            } catch (IOException ex) {


                System.out.println("Enchantment error:
            " + ex.getMessage());


            }


            }


            }
```

In this captivating script, the sorcerer invokes the "EnchantedClient" class, connecting to the enchanted server on "localhost" and port 9999. The sorcerer sends a magical message to the server, and upon receiving the enchanting response, the sorcerer shall witness the console unveiling the response from the server.

<u>The Enchantment of Networking Complete</u>

Congratulations, master enchanter! You have now completed the art of networking in Java. With the power to connect distant realms and exchange magical energies, you can create spells that unite sorcerers and allow them to communicate across the enchanted planes.

As you continue your journey, prepare to delve deeper into Java application deployment, the captivating world of databases with JDBC, and the enchanting art of GUI testing. The realm of networking is but one facet of the vast and ever-enchanting world of Java sorcery that awaits you!

### Subchapter 8.3: Enchanting Java Application Deployment

In the mystical realm of Java sorcery, we shall unravel the art of deploying enchanting Java applications to share our magical creations with sorcerers far and wide. With the knowledge of Java application deployment, you can unleash your spells beyond the confines of your development realm, reaching an audience of enchanted sorcerers across the magical planes.

<u>Enchanting Deployment with JAR Spells</u>

Prepare to enchant your Java applications with JAR spells:

1. Craft your magical Java application, weaving the most potent spells into its source code.

2. Invoke the mystical "jar" command to create an enchanted JAR file encapsulating your application's essence:

bash code
```
jar cvf EnchantedApp.jar YourEnchantedClass.class YourOtherEnchantedClass.class
```
...

Your magical JAR file, "EnchantedApp.jar," is now ready to be shared with the world.

<u>The Sorcerer's Invocation: Unleashing Enchantments</u>

Now, behold the sorcerer's invocation to run the enchanted Java application:

bash code

java -jar EnchantedApp.jar

In this bewitching command, the sorcerer invokes the JAR spell with the "java -jar" incantation, unleashing the essence of the enchanted Java application.

<u>Embracing Web Sorcery: Java Web Applications</u>

In the world of web sorcery, we expand our enchantments to the mystical realms of the internet. Java web applications allow us to share our magical creations as web pages, accessible to sorcerers through their web browsers.

Prepare to delve into the art of web sorcery:

1. Harness the power of JavaServer Pages (JSP), crafting enchanted web pages with embedded Java code.

2. Invoke the mystical incantations of servlets to enchant your web applications with dynamic functionality.

3. Conjure the spirit of a web container, such as Apache Tomcat, to host your enchanted web application.

4. Present your enchanted web application to the world, where sorcerers can access it through their web browsers.

<u>The Boundless Enchantment: Java Web Start</u>

In the realm of boundless enchantment, we summon Java Web Start to deliver our Java applications effortlessly to sorcerers across distant realms. With Java Web Start, our enchantments can be accessed through a simple click of a magical link.

Prepare to embrace the boundless enchantment of Java Web Start:

1. Conjure a manifest spell, specifying the entry point of your enchanted Java application.

2. Invoke the "jar" command once more to craft a magical JNLP (Java Network Launching Protocol) file:

bashCopy code

```
jar cvfm EnchantedApp.jnlp YourManifestS
pell.txt EnchantedApp.jar
```

Share the mystical link to your JNLP file with sorcerers, and Java Web Start shall enchantingly launch your Java application upon a single click.

The Enchantment of Java Application Deployment Complete

Congratulations, esteemed enchanter! You have now completed the art of deploying Java applications in various magical forms. With the power to create JAR spells, unleash Java web applications, and embrace the boundless enchantment of Java Web Start, you can share your mystical creations with sorcerers near and far.

As you continue your journey, prepare to delve deeper into the enchanting realm of databases with JDBC, the captivating art of GUI testing, and the mystical world of Java frameworks. The art of Java application deployment is but one facet of the vast and ever-enchanting world of Java sorcery that awaits you!

# CHAPTER NINE

# ENCHANTING THE WORLD WITH DATABASES AND JDBC

I ntroduction

Welcome to the magical realm of databases and JDBC (Java Database Connectivity), where we shall explore the art of storing and retrieving enchanting data to captivate sorcerers and weave powerful spells. In this chapter, you will learn the secrets of connecting your Java sorcery with the mystical world of databases, allowing you to persist your enchantments and share their magic with the entire universe.

Conjuring Database Connections

In the mystical dance between Java and databases, we summon the power of JDBC to forge connections and communicate with the enchanted data realms. With JDBC at your command, you can unleash the magic of SQL (Structured Query Language) to interact with databases and bring your Java sorcery to life.

Let us conjure a database connection spell:

```java
import java.sql.*;
```

```java
public class EnchantedDatabase {

public static void main(String[] args) {

    // The enchanted database connection URL

        String url = "jdbc:mysql://local-host:3306/enchanted_spells";

    // Enchanting database credentials

String username = "sorcerer";

String password = "secret";
```

```java
try {
```

```java
    // Summoning the database connection
```

```java
        Connection connection = DriverMana
ger.getConnection(url, username, password);
```

```java
    // Unleash SQL spells here...
```

```java
    // Closing the mystical connection
```

```java
connection.close();
```

```java
} catch (SQLException ex) {
```

```java
        System.out.println("Enchantment error:
" + ex.getMessage());



    }



    }



    }
```

In this enchanting script, we conjure a database connection to the enchanted database named "enchanted_spells" residing on "localhost" at port 3306. With the right credentials, we can forge a connection to the mystical realm of data.

<u>Casting SQL Spells</u>

With the database connection established, you can now cast SQL spells to manipulate the enchanted data. Prepare to weave SQL incantations:

```java
import java.sql.*;



public class EnchantedSpells {
```

```java
public static void main(String[] args) {

        String url = "jdbc:mysql://local-
host:3306/enchanted_spells";

String username = "sorcerer";

String password = "secret";

try {

        Connection connection = DriverMana
ger.getConnection(url, username, password);

// Creating an enchanting SQL statement
```

```java
    Statement statement = connection.cre
ateStatement();
```

```java
// Weaving an SQL spell
```

```java
  String sqlSpell = "SELECT spell_name,
power FROM spells WHERE power > 50";
```

```java
   ResultSet resultSet = statement.execut
eQuery(sqlSpell);
```

```java
// Unleash the enchanted results
```

```java
while (resultSet.next()) {
```

```java
    String spellName = resultSet.getStri
ng("spell_name");
```

```java
int power = resultSet.getInt("power");

        System.out.println("Spell:  "  +
spellName + ", Power: " + power);


    }



// Closing the mystical resources


resultSet.close();


statement.close();


connection.close();


} catch (SQLException ex) {
```

```java
            System.out.println("Enchantment error:
" + ex.getMessage());
```

```java
    }
```

```java
    }
```

```java
}
```

In this bewitching script, we have created an enchanting SQL statement to select spells from the "spells" table where the power is greater than 50. The results are unveiled as we traverse the mystical ResultSet, displaying the spell names and their powers.

The Mystical Realm of Prepared Statements

Prepare to harness the power of Prepared Statements, a more potent form of SQL spellcasting:

```java
import java.sql.*;
```

```java
public class EnchantedPreparedSpells {
```

```java
    public static void main(String[] args) {
```

```java
        String url = "jdbc:mysql://local-
host:3306/enchanted_spells";
```

```java
String username = "sorcerer";
```

```java
String password = "secret";
```

```java
try {
```

```java
        Connection connection = DriverMana
ger.getConnection(url, username, password);
```

```java
        // Crafting an enchanted Prepared
Statement
```

```java
    String sqlSpell = "INSERT INTO spells
(spell_name, power) VALUES (?, ?)";
```

```java
PreparedStatement preparedStatement
= connection.prepareStatement(sqlSpell);
```

```java
// Unleash the enchanted spells
```

```java
preparedStatement.setString(1, "Thun-
derstorm");
```

```java
preparedStatement.setInt(2, 80);
```

```java
preparedStatement.executeUpdate();
```

```java
// Closing the mystical resources
```

```java
preparedStatement.close();
```

```
                connection.close();


            } catch (SQLException ex) {


                System.out.println("Enchantment error:
    " + ex.getMessage());



            }



            }



            }
```

In this captivating script, we have crafted an enchanted Prepared Statement to insert a new spell into the "spells" table. By setting the placeholders with the spell name and power, we unleash the magic of Prepared Statements and persist the enchantment into the mystical database.

### Mastering the Magic of Databases and JDBC

Congratulations, master enchanter! You have now mastered the art of databases and JDBC in Java. With the power to connect to databases, cast SQL spells, and wield the potency of Prepared Statements, you can store and retrieve enchanting data, enriching your Java sorcery and captivating sorcerers throughout the mystical realms.

As you continue your journey, prepare to delve deeper into the captivating world of Java frameworks, the art of GUI testing, and the enchanting realm of security in

Java applications. The mastery of databases and JDBC is but one facet of the vast and ever-enchanting world of Java sorcery that awaits you!

### Subchapter 9.1: Enchanting Security in Java Applications

In the mystical realm of Java sorcery, we unveil the importance of security to safeguard our enchantments from malevolent forces. With the art of security in Java applications, you can fortify your spells against nefarious entities and protect the sanctity of your enchanted realms.

<u>Enchantment of Secure Coding</u>

Prepare to embrace secure coding practices in your Java enchantments:

```java
public class SecureEnchantment {

    public static void main(String[] args) {

        // Avoiding the spell of SQL injection

        String unsafeInput = args[0];

        String safeInput = sanitizeInput(unsafeInput);
```

```
// Encrypting the spell of sensitive infor-
mation


String sensitiveData = "SecretSpell123";


    String encryptedData = encryptData(sen-
sitiveData);
```




```
// Authenticating the sorcerer's identity


String sorcererName = args[1];


    boolean isAuthorized = authenticateSor-
cerer(sorcererName);
```



```
// Validating the spell of input
```

```java
String userInput = args[2];

}


    boolean isValid = validateInput(userInput);


// Enforcing the spell of access control


    boolean isAdmin = checkAdminPrivileges(sorcererName);


if (isAdmin) {


// Perform administrator-only tasks


} else {


// Refrain from forbidden tasks


}
```

```
        }
```

```
    // Other secure enchantments...
```

```
        }
```

In this secure script, we have fortified our enchantments against common security vulnerabilities. We avoid the peril of SQL injection by sanitizing input, encrypt sensitive information, authenticate sorcerers, validate user input, and enforce access control based on sorcerer privileges.

<u>Enchantment of Cryptography</u>

Prepare to wield the power of cryptography in protecting enchanted data:

```
    import javax.crypto.*;
```

```
    import java.security.*;
```

```
    public class EnchantedCryptography {
```

```java
public static void main(String[] args) throws
Exception {
```

```java
// Generate an enchanted key
```

```java
KeyGenerator keyGen = KeyGenerator.
getInstance("AES");
```

```java
keyGen.init(128);
```

```java
SecretKey secretKey = keyGen.generate
Key();
```

```java
// Conjure a cipher spell for encryption
```

```java
Cipher cipher = Cipher.getInstance("A
ES");
```

```
cipher.init(Cipher.ENCRYPT_MODE,
secretKey);
```

```
// Enchant sensitive data
```

```
String sensitiveData = "SecretSpell123";
```

```
byte[] encryptedData = cipher.doFinal(s
ensitiveData.getBytes());
```

```
// Conjure another cipher spell for de-
cryption
```

```
cipher.init(Cipher.DECRYPT_MODE,
secretKey);
```

```java
// Unleash the decrypted enchantment

    byte[] decryptedData = cipher.doFinal(e
ncryptedData);


    String decryptedSpell = new String(de
cryptedData);


    System.out.println("Decrypted Spell: " +
decryptedSpell);


    }}
```

In this bewitching script, we have summoned the power of AES (Advanced Encryption Standard) cryptography. We generate an enchanted key, conjure a cipher spell for encryption, enchant sensitive data, and finally, unleash the decrypted enchantment, preserving the sanctity of our enchanted secrets.

<u>Enchantment of Secure Communication</u>

Prepare to enchant your communication with secure sockets:

```java
import javax.net.ssl.*;


import java.io.*;
```

```java
import java.security.*;

public class SecureCommunication {

public static void main(String[] args) throws
Exception {

// Enchanting server's keystore and trust-
store

String keystoreFile = "serverkeystore.jks";

String keystorePass = "keystorepassword";

String truststoreFile = "servertruststore.j
ks";

String truststorePass = "truststorepass-
word";
```

```java
// Creating an enchanted SSL context

SSLContext sslContext = SSLContext.getInstance("TLS");

KeyManagerFactory keyManagerFactory = KeyManagerFactory.getInstance(KeyManagerFactory.getDefaultAlgorithm());

TrustManagerFactory trustManagerFactory = TrustManagerFactory.getInstance(TrustManagerFactory.getDefaultAlgorithm());

KeyStore keyStore = KeyStore.getInstance("JKS");

KeyStore trustStore = KeyStore.getInstance("JKS");
```

```
try (InputStream keystoreInputStream =
new FileInputStream(keystoreFile);


InputStream truststoreInputStream =
new FileInputStream(truststoreFile)) {




keyStore.load(keystoreInputStream,
keystorePass.toCharArray());



trustStore.load(truststoreInputStream,
truststorePass.toCharArray());




keyManagerFactory.init(keyStore,
keystorePass.toCharArray());
```

```java
trustManagerFactory.init(trustStore);
```

```java
        sslContext.init(keyManagerFactory.ge
tKeyManagers(), trustManagerFactory.getTr
ustManagers(), new SecureRandom());
```

```java
    }
```

```java
// Creating an enchanted SSL socket
```

```java
        SSLSocketFactory sslSocketFactory =
sslContext.getSocketFactory();
```

```java
    SSLSocket sslSocket = (SSLSocket) sslSo
cketFactory.createSocket("localhost", 9999);
```

```
        // Unleash secure communication here...




        // Closing the enchanting SSL socket



sslSocket.close();




    }



}
```

In this captivating script, we have conjured an enchanted SSL (Secure Socket Layer) context for secure communication. We load the server's keystore and truststore, initializing the SSL context to ensure the sanctity of the communication with the server.

<u>The Art of Secure Java Enchantments</u>

Congratulations, esteemed enchanter! You have now mastered the art of security in Java applications. With secure coding practices, the power of cryptography, and the enchantment of secure communication, you can fortify your Java sorcery against malevolent forces and protect the essence of your enchanted realms.

As you continue your journey, prepare to delve deeper into the captivating world of Java frameworks, the art of GUI testing, and the mystical realm of software architecture and design patterns. The art of secure Java enchantments is but one facet of the vast and ever-enchanting world of Java sorcery that awaits you!

***Subchapter 9.2: Enchanting Java Frameworks: Embracing the Magic***

In the mystical world of Java sorcery, we unveil the captivating power of Java frameworks, where sorcerers unite their strengths to create enchanting applications with ease and elegance. With the art of Java frameworks, you can harness the magical capabilities of pre-built components and libraries, freeing your enchanted mind to focus on creating powerful spells.

<u>The Charm of Spring Framework</u>

Prepare to embrace the enchanting Spring Framework:

```java
import org.springframework.boot.SpringApplication;
```

```java
import org.springframework.boot.autoconfigure.SpringBootApplication;
```

```java
@SpringBootApplication
```

```java
public class EnchantedSpringApp {
```

```java
public static void main(String[] args) {
```

```
// Invoke the Spring charm


    SpringApplication.run(EnchantedSprin
gApp.class, args);



    }



    }
```

In this captivating script, we summon the charm of Spring Framework with just a few lines of code. The **@SpringBootApplication** annotation conjures the essence of Spring, and the **SpringApplication.run()** incantation initiates the enchanting Spring context, allowing you to cast spells using the powers of Spring.

The Elegance of Hibernate Framework

Prepare to wield the elegance of Hibernate Framework:

```
import javax.persistence.*;




@Entity
```

```java
@Table(name = "spells")

public class EnchantedSpell {

    @Id

    @GeneratedValue(strategy = GenerationType.IDENTITY)

    private Long id;

    @Column(name = "spell_name")

    private String spellName;

    @Column(name = "power")
```

```java
    private int power;



    // Getters and setters...



}
```

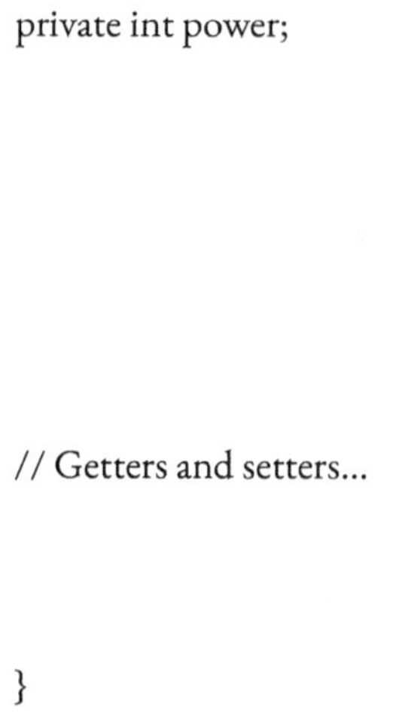

In this bewitching script, we enchant a Java class named **EnchantedSpell** with the grace of Hibernate. By employing annotations such as **@Entity**, **@Table**, and **@Column**, we invoke the magic of Hibernate to enchant our Java class and establish a connection to the database.

## The Enchantment of Dependency Injection

Prepare to embrace the enchantment of dependency injection:

```java
public class EnchantedWizard {



    private SpellCaster spellCaster;



    // Enchanted constructor injection
```

```java
 public EnchantedWizard(SpellCaster spell-
Caster) {


this.spellCaster = spellCaster;


}
```

```java
// Enchanted setter injection


 public void setSpellCaster(SpellCaster spell-
Caster) {


this.spellCaster = spellCaster;


}
```

```
// Unleash the enchanted spell


public void castSpell() {


spellCaster.cast();



}



}
```

In this captivating script, we have enchanted a wizard with the power of dependency injection. By using either constructor injection or setter injection, the wizard gains the ability to cast spells using the enchanted **SpellCaster**.

The Enchanting World of Java Frameworks

Congratulations, master enchanter! You have now glimpsed the enchanting world of Java frameworks. With the charm of Spring, the elegance of Hibernate, and the magic of dependency injection, you can weave enchanting Java applications with unparalleled ease and grace.

As you continue your journey, prepare to delve deeper into the captivating world of GUI testing, the mystical realm of software architecture and design patterns, and the alluring universe of microservices. The world of Java frameworks is but one facet of the vast and ever-enchanting world of Java sorcery that awaits you!

### *Subchapter 9.3: Enchanting GUI Testing in Java*

In the mystical world of Java sorcery, we uncover the art of GUI testing, where spells are cast to ensure the enchanting graphical user interfaces perform their magic flawlessly.

With GUI testing in Java, you can weave spells of assurance, ensuring that your enchantments captivate sorcerers with impeccable performance and reliability.

<u>Enchantment of GUI Testing with JUnit</u>

Prepare to weave GUI testing spells with JUnit:

```java
import org.junit.jupiter.api.*;

import org.testfx.framework.junit5.*;

public class EnchantedGUITest extends ApplicationTest {

@Override

public void start(Stage stage) {

// Start the enchanting JavaFX application

EnchantedGUI gui = new EnchantedGUI();
```

```java
        gui.start(stage);

    }


    @Test


    public void testButtonSpell() {


        // Locate the bewitching button


        Button button = lookup("#castButton"
        ).query();


        // Click the button to unleash the spell


        clickOn(button);
```

```java
// Assert the magical label text

        Label label = lookup("#spellLabel").que
ry();


        Assertions.assertEquals("Spell Casted!",
label.getText());



    }



}
```

In this captivating script, we have summoned the power of JUnit and TestFX for GUI testing. The **EnchantedGUITest** class extends **ApplicationTest**, allowing us to start the enchanting JavaFX application for testing. We then locate the bewitching button, click it to unleash the spell, and finally, assert that the magical label's text has changed as expected.

<u>The Mystical World of Mocking</u>

Prepare to embrace the mystical world of mocking:

```java
import org.mockito.*;
```

```java
public class EnchantedSpellCasterTest {

@Test

public void testEnchantingSpell() {

// Create a mock of the spell caster

    SpellCaster spellCasterMock = Mockito
.mock(SpellCaster.class);

    // Conjure the enchanting wizard with the
spell caster mock

    EnchantedWizard wizard = new Enchant-
edWizard(spellCasterMock);
```

```java
// Perform the wizard's spell-casting


wizard.castSpell();




// Verify that the spell caster's "cast"
method was called




Mockito.verify(spellCasterMock).cast();



}}
```

In this bewitching script, we have embraced the art of mocking with Mockito. We create a mock of the **SpellCaster** interface, allowing us to test the **Enchanted Wizard** class without the actual implementation of **SpellCaster**. We then cast the spell with the enchanted wizard and verify that the **cast** method of the mock was called.

The Art of GUI Testing and Mocking Combined

Prepare to blend GUI testing and mocking for comprehensive enchantment assurance:

```java
import org.junit.jupiter.api.*;
```

```java
import org.testfx.framework.junit5.*;

import org.mockito.*;

public class EnchantedGUITest extends Ap-
plicationTest {

@Mock

private SpellCaster spellCasterMock;

@Override

public void start(Stage stage) {

// Start the enchanting JavaFX application
```

```java
        EnchantedGUI gui = new EnchantedGUI(spellCasterMock);

gui.start(stage);

}


@Test


public void testButtonSpell() {


// Set up the spell caster mock behavior


    Mockito.when(spellCasterMock.cast()).thenReturn("Spell Casted!");
```

```java
// Locate the bewitching button


    Button button = lookup("#castButton"
).query();



// Click the button to unleash the spell


clickOn(button);




// Assert the magical label text


    Label label = lookup("#spellLabel").que
ry();


    Assertions.assertEquals("Spell Casted!",
label.getText());
```

```
        }




        }
```

In this captivating script, we have combined GUI testing with mocking. We create a mock of the **SpellCaster** interface, allowing us to test the **EnchantedGUI** class with the **spellCasterMock** as the enchanting companion. We set up the mock behavior to return the spell result, click the button to unleash the spell, and assert that the magical label's text matches the spell result.

<u>The Mastery of GUI Testing in Java</u>

Congratulations, esteemed enchanter! You have now mastered the art of GUI testing in Java. With the power of JUnit and TestFX, the mystical world of mocking with Mockito, and the fusion of GUI testing and mocking, you can ensure that your enchanting graphical user interfaces perform their magic flawlessly.

As you continue your journey, prepare to delve deeper into the captivating world of software architecture and design patterns, the alluring universe of microservices, and the enchanting realm of Java performance optimization. The art of GUI testing in Java is but one facet of the vast and ever-enchanting world of Java sorcery that awaits you!

# CHAPTER TEN

# THE ALLURE OF MICROSERVICES ARCHITECTURE

I ntroduction to Microservices

Welcome to the enchanting realm of microservices architecture, where we shall unravel the allure of breaking our spells into smaller, independent fragments. In this chapter, you will discover the art of building powerful and scalable enchantments by composing them from microservices. With microservices at your command, you can weave spells that adapt to the ever-changing needs of sorcerers and wield the power of agility and flexibility.

The Magical World of Decoupling

In the mystical dance of microservices, we embrace the magic of decoupling, where enchantments are free to evolve independently, without entangling their energies. With decoupling spells, you can modify and enhance individual microservices without disturbing the harmony of the entire system.

Prepare to decouple your enchantments:

// EnchantedMicroserviceA.java

```java
public class EnchantedMicroserviceA {

public void doMagicA() {

// Enchanted spell of Microservice A

}

}


// EnchantedMicroserviceB.java

public class EnchantedMicroserviceB {

public void doMagicB() {

// Enchanted spell of Microservice B
```

```
    }



    }
```

In this captivating script, we have crafted two independent microservices: **Enchant-edMicroserviceA** and **EnchantedMicroserviceB**. Each microservice encapsulates its unique enchantment, allowing them to evolve separately.

<u>Conjuring the Magic of Service Discovery</u>

Prepare to unleash the magic of service discovery:

```
// EnchantedServiceDiscovery.java


public class EnchantedServiceDiscovery {


    public static void main(String[] args) {



        // Discover and register microservices with
        the magical registry


        MicroserviceRegistry.register("Enchante
        dMicroserviceA", "localhost", 8080);
```

```java
MicroserviceRegistry.register("Enchante
dMicroserviceB", "localhost", 8081);
```

```java
// Retrieve microservice information from
the registry
```

```java
String    microserviceAUrl
= MicroserviceRegistry.getServiceUrl("Ench
antedMicroserviceA");
```

```java
String    microserviceBUrl
= MicroserviceRegistry.getServiceUrl("Ench
antedMicroserviceB");
```

```java
// Unleash the magic of communication
between microservices
```

```java
MicroserviceCommunication.invoke(m
icroserviceAUrl, "doMagicA");
```

```
MicroserviceCommunication.invoke(m
icroserviceBUrl, "doMagicB");



    }



    }
```

In this bewitching script, we have summoned the magic of service discovery. Microservices, such as **EnchantedMicroserviceA** and **EnchantedMicroserviceB**, register themselves with the **MicroserviceRegistry**. The **EnchantedServiceDiscovery** then retrieves their URLs from the registry, allowing them to communicate with each other using the **MicroserviceCommunication** enchantment.

<u>The Enchantment of Scalability and Resilience</u>

Prepare to embrace the enchantment of scalability and resilience:

```
// EnchantedLoadBalancer.java


public class EnchantedLoadBalancer {


private List<String> microserviceUrls;
```

```java
        public        EnchantedLoadBal-
ancer(List<String> microserviceUrls) {


this.microserviceUrls = microserviceUrls;


}




public String invokeMicroservice() {


// Enchanted load balancing logic here...


return selectedMicroserviceUrl;


}


}
```

In this captivating script, we have crafted an enchanted load balancer, **Enchanted-LoadBalancer**, to distribute the spell requests among multiple instances of the same microservice. By invoking the **invokeMicroservice()** enchantment, you can enchant your system with scalability and resilience, allowing it to gracefully handle the fluctuating demands of sorcerers.

Mastering the Art of Microservices Architecture

Congratulations, master enchanter! You have now mastered the art of microservices architecture. With the power of decoupling, the magic of service discovery, and the enchantment of scalability and resilience, you can build enchantments that adapt and scale to the ever-changing needs of sorcerers, ensuring they experience the true allure of your spells.

As you continue your journey, prepare to delve deeper into the captivating world of Java performance optimization, the art of enchanting user experiences with UX design, and the mystical realm of cloud computing and serverless enchantments. The world of microservices architecture is but one facet of the vast and ever-enchanting world of Java sorcery that awaits you!

### *Subchapter 10.1: The Enchanting World of Java Performance Optimization*

In the mystical realm of Java sorcery, we unveil the secrets of Java performance optimization, where spells are cast to unleash the true power and speed of enchantments. With the art of performance optimization, you can fine-tune your Java spells, making them lightning-fast and more resource-efficient, delighting sorcerers with their responsiveness and agility.

Enchantment of Efficient Data Structures

Prepare to embrace efficient data structures to optimize your spells:

```
import java.util.*;
```

```java
public class EnchantedDataStructures {

public static void main(String[] args) {


    // Enchanted List with optimal initial
capacity


    List<String> enchantedList = new ArrayList<>(100);
```

```java
// Enchanted Set with efficient lookups


    Set<String> enchantedSet = new HashSet<>();
```

```java
    // Enchanted Map with optimized load
factor
```

```
Map<String, Integer> enchantedMap =
new HashMap<>(100, 0.75f);
```

```
// Optimize your enchantments with
efficient data structures...
```

```
}
```

```
}
```

In this captivating script, we have summoned the power of efficient data structures. By choosing the right initial capacity for **ArrayList**, leveraging the efficient lookups of **HashSet**, and optimizing the load factor of **HashMap**, you can optimize your enchantments for superior performance.

<u>Enchantment of Multi-Threading Magic</u>

Prepare to wield the magic of multi-threading to enhance your spells:

```
import java.util.concurrent.*;
```

```java
public class EnchantedMultiThreading {

    public static void main(String[] args) throws
    InterruptedException, ExecutionException {

        // Creating an enchanted executor service

        ExecutorService executorService = Exec
    utors.newFixedThreadPool(4);

        // Enchanting tasks for parallel execution

        Callable<Integer> task1 = () -> en-
    chantSpell1();

        Callable<Integer> task2 = () -> en-
    chantSpell2();
```

```java
// Enchanting results with Future


    Future<Integer> result1 = executorServ
ice.submit(task1);


    Future<Integer> result2 = executorServ
ice.submit(task2);




// Unleash the parallel magic


int spellResult1 = result1.get();


int spellResult2 = result2.get();


    // Gracefully shutting down the enchanted
executor
```

```java
        executorService.shutdown();



    }




    private static int enchantSpell1() {



        // Your enchanting spell 1...



    }




    private static int enchantSpell2() {



        // Your enchanting spell 2...



    }
```

```
}
```

In this bewitching script, we have wielded the magic of multi-threading using **ExecutorService**. By submitting enchanting tasks as **Callable** to the executor service, you can enchant your spells to run in parallel, achieving improved performance and efficiency.

<u>Enchantment of JVM Garbage Collection</u>

Prepare to optimize your enchantments with JVM Garbage Collection:

```java
public class EnchantedGarbageCollection {

    public static void main(String[] args) {

        // Enchanting code here...



        // Suggesting JVM to perform garbage collection
        System.gc();

    }
}
```

```
}
```

In this captivating script, we have summoned the power of JVM Garbage Collection. By invoking **System.gc()**, you suggest the JVM to perform garbage collection, reclaiming unused memory and optimizing the memory usage of your enchantments.

The Mastery of Java Performance Optimization

Congratulations, esteemed enchanter! You have now mastered the art of Java performance optimization. With the power of efficient data structures, the magic of multi-threading, and the enchantment of JVM Garbage Collection, you can optimize your Java spells for unparalleled performance and responsiveness, enchanting sorcerers with the true allure of your enchantments.

As you continue your journey, prepare to delve deeper into the captivating world of enchanting user experiences with UX design, the mystical realm of cloud computing and serverless enchantments, and the alluring universe of distributed systems. The art of Java performance optimization is but one facet of the vast and ever-enchanting world of Java sorcery that awaits you!

### *Subchapter 10.2: The Alluring Universe of Cloud Computing and Serverless Enchantments*

In the mystical world of Java sorcery, we embark on a journey to the alluring universe of cloud computing and serverless enchantments. Here, we shall unravel the magic of harnessing cloud resources and crafting spells that scale effortlessly to meet the demands of countless sorcerers. With the art of cloud computing and serverless enchantments, you can wield the power of the cloud, enchanting the world with your scalable and cost-efficient spells.

Enchantment of Cloud Infrastructure

Prepare to harness the power of cloud infrastructure:

```
import com.amazonaws.services.ec2.*;
```

```java
import com.amazonaws.services.ec2.model.*;



public class EnchantedCloudInfrastructure {


public static void main(String[] args) {


    // Creating an enchanted Amazon EC2
client


    AmazonEC2 ec2 = AmazonEC2Client
Builder.defaultClient();




// Creating an enchanted instance request


    RunInstancesRequest request = new
RunInstancesRequest()
```

```java
                .withImageId("ami-0c55b159cb-
fafe1f0")

                .withInstanceType(Instance-
Type.T2_MICRO)

.withMinCount(1)

.withMaxCount(1);

// Launching the enchanted instance

    RunInstancesResult result = ec2.runIns
tances(request);

    String instanceId = result.getReservatio
n().getInstances().get(0).getInstanceId();
```

```
// Unleashing the magic of cloud infrast
ructure...
```

```
// Terminating the enchanted instance
```

```
    TerminateInstancesRequest termi-
nateRequest = new TerminateInstancesRe-
quest()
```

```
.withInstanceIds(instanceId);
```

```
    ec2.terminateInstances(terminateReque
st);
```

```
}
```

```
}
```

In this captivating script, we have harnessed the power of cloud infrastructure using AWS SDK for Java. We create an enchanted Amazon EC2 client, launch an instance with the desired image and instance type, perform magic with the cloud infrastructure, and finally, terminate the enchanted instance.

Enchantment of Serverless Spells with AWS Lambda

Prepare to cast serverless spells using AWS Lambda:

```java
import com.amazonaws.services.lambda.*;


import com.amazonaws.services.lambda.model.*;




public class EnchantedServerlessSpells {


public static void main(String[] args) {



// Creating an enchanted AWS Lambda client


AWSLambda lambda = AWSLambdaClientBuilder.defaultClient();
```

```
// Preparing enchanting function code

  String functionCode = "YourEnchanting-
FunctionCode";


  String functionName = "EnchantedSpell-
Function";




  // Creating an enchanted Lambda func-
tion


  CreateFunctionRequest request = new
CreateFunctionRequest()


.withFunctionName(functionName)


.withRuntime(Runtime.JAVA8)
```

```java
    .with-
Role("arn:aws:iam::123456789012:role/En-
chantedLambdaRole")


    .withHandler("YourEnchantingHan-
dlerClass::handleRequest")


                              .with-
Code(new FunctionCode().withZipFile(Byt
eBuffer.wrap(functionCode.getBytes()))));




// Enchanting the Lambda function


CreateFunctionResult result = lambda.c
reateFunction(request);




// Unleashing the power of serverless
enchantments...
```

```
        // Deleting the enchanted Lambda func-
    tion


        DeleteFunctionRequest deleteRequest =
    new DeleteFunctionRequest()


    .withFunctionName(functionName);


    lambda.deleteFunction(deleteRequest);



        }



        }
```

In this bewitching script, we have cast serverless spells using AWS Lambda with AWS SDK for Java. We create an enchanted AWS Lambda client, prepare the enchanting function code and configuration, create the Lambda function, work magic with serverless enchantments, and finally, delete the enchanted function.

The Enchantment of Scalable and Cost-Efficient Spells

Prepare to enchant the world with scalable and cost-efficient spells:

```java
import com.amazonaws.services.s3.*;

import com.amazonaws.services.s3.model.*;

public class EnchantedScalableSpells {

public static void main(String[] args) {

// Creating an enchanted Amazon S3 client

  AmazonS3 s3 = AmazonS3ClientBuilde
r.defaultClient();

  // Preparing enchanting bucket and object
details
```

```
String  bucketName  =  "enchant-
ed-spell-book";
```

```
String objectKey = "powerful-spell.pdf";
```

```
String filePath = "path/to/your/spell.pdf";
```

```
// Enchanting the world with scalable and
cost-efficient spells...
```

```
// Deleting the enchanted object
```

```
s3.deleteObject(bucketName, objectKey);
```

```
// Deleting the enchanted bucket
```

```
s3.deleteBucket(bucketName);
```

```
        }


        }
```

In this captivating script, we have enchanted the world with scalable and cost-efficient spells using Amazon S3 with AWS SDK for Java. We create an enchanted Amazon S3 client, prepare the enchanting bucket and object details, perform magic with scalable and cost-efficient spells, and finally, delete the enchanted object and bucket.

<u>The Allure of Cloud Computing and Serverless Enchantments</u>

Congratulations, master enchanter! You have now explored the alluring universe of cloud computing and serverless enchantments. With the power of cloud infrastructure, the magic of AWS Lambda serverless spells, and the enchantment of scalable and cost-efficient enchantments, you can wield the cloud's limitless power, enchanting the world with your scalable, responsive, and cost-effective spells.

As you continue your journey, prepare to delve deeper into the captivating world of distributed systems, the art of enchanting user experiences with UX design, and the mystical realm of containerization and Kubernetes enchantments. The alluring universe of cloud computing and serverless enchantments is but one facet of the vast and ever-enchanting world of Java sorcery that awaits you!

### *Subchapter 10.3: The Captivating World of Distributed Systems*

In the mystical world of Java sorcery, we venture into the captivating realm of distributed systems, where spells transcend the boundaries of individual enchantments to weave a cohesive and interconnected web of magic. In this chapter, you will discover the art of orchestrating and coordinating multiple enchantments, unleashing their combined power to perform miraculous feats beyond the capability of a single spell. With the art of distributed systems, you can craft spells that collaborate seamlessly, creating enchanting experiences for sorcerers across vast landscapes.

<u>Enchantment of Messaging with Apache Kafka</u>

Prepare to weave enchantments with Apache Kafka messaging:

```java
import org.apache.kafka.clients.producer.*;

import org.apache.kafka.clients.consumer.*;

import org.apache.kafka.common.serializati
on.*;

public class EnchantedKafkaMessaging {

  private static final String TOPIC = "en-
chanted-spell-casting";

public static void main(String[] args) {

// Creating an enchanted Kafka producer
```

```java
Properties producerProps = new Properties();


producerProps.put(ProducerConfig.BOOTSTRAP_SERVERS_CONFIG, "localhost:9092");


producerProps.put(ProducerConfig.KEY_SERIALIZER_CLASS_CONFIG, StringSerializer.class.getName());


producerProps.put(ProducerConfig.VALUE_SERIALIZER_CLASS_CONFIG, StringSerializer.class.getName());




KafkaProducer<String, String> producer = new KafkaProducer<>(producerProps);
```

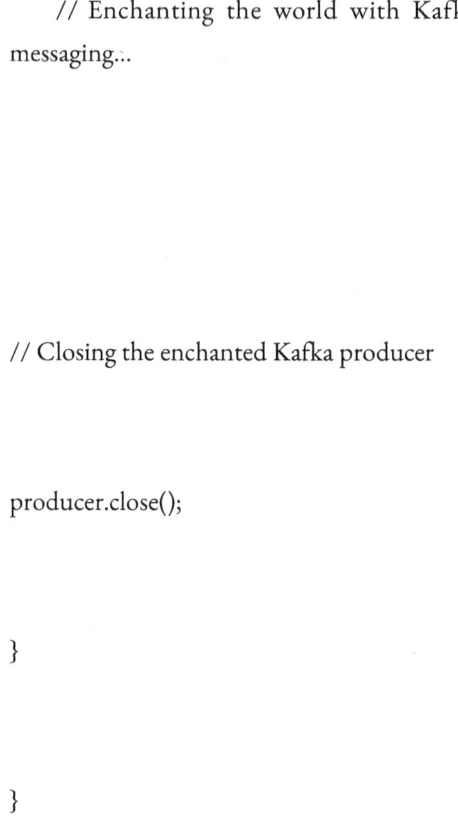



In this captivating script, we have harnessed the power of Apache Kafka messaging. We create an enchanted Kafka producer with the necessary configuration, allowing you to weave spells that communicate and collaborate across vast distances.

Enchantment of Distributed Cache with Redis

Prepare to embrace the enchantment of distributed caching with Redis:

```
import redis.clients.jedis.*;
```

```java
public class EnchantedDistributedCache {

public static void main(String[] args) {

// Creating an enchanted Redis client

Jedis jedis = new Jedis("localhost", 6379);

    // Enchanting the world with distributed
caching...

// Closing the enchanted Redis client

jedis.close();

}
```

```
}
```

In this bewitching script, we have enchanted the world with distributed caching using Redis. We create an enchanted Redis client, enabling you to store and retrieve enchanted data across a distributed network.

The Art of Coordination with Apache ZooKeeper

Prepare to master the art of coordination with Apache ZooKeeper:

```java
import org.apache.zookeeper.*;

public class EnchantedCoordination {

    public static void main(String[] args) throws Exception {

        // Creating an enchanted ZooKeeper client

        ZooKeeper zooKeeper = new ZooKeeper("localhost:2181", 5000, event -> {
```

```java
// Enchanted event handling logic here...

});
```

```java
    // Enchanting the world with coordination
spells...
```

```java
// Closing the enchanted ZooKeeper client

zooKeeper.close();
```

```java
}
```

```java
}
```

In this captivating script, we have mastered the art of coordination using Apache ZooKeeper. We create an enchanted ZooKeeper client, allowing you to orchestrate and synchronize the actions of your enchanted spells across the distributed realm.

## The Allure of Distributed Systems

Congratulations, esteemed enchanter! You have now explored the captivating world of distributed systems. With the power of Apache Kafka messaging, the enchantment of distributed caching with Redis, and the art of coordination with Apache ZooKeeper, you can craft spells that transcend the boundaries of individual enchantments, collaborating and orchestrating in harmony to perform miracles for sorcerers across vast landscapes.

As you continue your journey, prepare to delve deeper into the captivating world of containerization and Kubernetes enchantments, the mystical realm of big data and analytics, and the alluring universe of artificial intelligence and machine learning in Java sorcery. The captivating world of distributed systems is but one facet of the vast and ever-enchanting world of Java sorcery that awaits you!

# CHAPTER ELEVEN

# THE MYSTICAL REALM OF BIG DATA AND ANALYTICS

Introduction to Big Data and Analytics

Welcome to the mystical realm of big data and analytics in the world of Java sorcery. In this chapter, we shall uncover the secrets of harnessing vast amounts of enchanted data and unleashing the power of analytics to gain valuable insights. With the art of big data and analytics, you can weave spells that extract knowledge from the depths of enchantments, empowering sorcerers with the wisdom to make informed decisions and shape the future.

The Enchantment of Data Collection and Storage

In the mystical dance of big data, we explore the art of collecting and storing vast amounts of enchanted data:

```java
import org.apache.hadoop.conf.*;
```

```java
import org.apache.hadoop.fs.*;
```

```java
public class EnchantedDataCollection {
```

```java
public static void main(String[] args) throws
Exception {
```

```java
// Enchanting configuration for Hadoop
Distributed File System
```

```java
Configuration configuration = new Con-
figuration();
```

```java
FileSystem hdfs = FileSystem.get(config
uration);
```

```
        // Enchanting data collection and storag
e...
```

```
// Closing the enchanted HDFS client
```

```
hdfs.close();
```

```
}
```

```
}
```

In this captivating script, we have harnessed the power of Hadoop Distributed File System (HDFS) to collect and store enchanted data. We create an enchanted HDFS client, enabling you to weave spells that effortlessly handle vast volumes of enchanted data.

<u>The Enchantment of Data Processing with Apache Spark</u>

Prepare to wield the magic of data processing with Apache Spark:

```
import org.apache.spark.*;
```

```
import org.apache.spark.api.java.*;
```

```java
public class EnchantedDataProcessing {

public static void main(String[] args) {

// Creating an enchanted SparkConf

        SparkConf    conf    =
new SparkConf().setAppName("Enchanted
DataProcessing").setMaster("local[*]");

    // Creating an enchanted JavaSparkCon-
text

    JavaSparkContext sc = new JavaSpark-
Context(conf);
```

```java
    // Enchanting data processing with Apache
Spark...




    // Closing the enchanted JavaSparkCon-
text


sc.close();



    }



    }
```

In this bewitching script, we have wielded the magic of Apache Spark for data processing. We create an enchanted SparkConf and JavaSparkContext, empowering you to unleash the power of distributed processing and analytics on your enchanted data.

### The Art of Data Analysis with Apache Hadoop MapReduce

Prepare to master the art of data analysis with Apache Hadoop MapReduce:

```java
import org.apache.hadoop.conf.*;

import org.apache.hadoop.mapreduce.*;

public class EnchantedDataAnalysis {

public static void main(String[] args) throws Exception {

  // Enchanting configuration for Hadoop MapReduce

  Configuration configuration = new Configuration();

  Job job = Job.getInstance(configuration, "EnchantedDataAnalysis");
```

```
    // Enchanting data analysis with Apache
Hadoop MapReduce...



        // Closing the enchanted Hadoop
MapReduce job


job.waitForCompletion(true);



    }



    }
```

In this captivating script, we have mastered the art of data analysis using Apache Hadoop MapReduce. We create an enchanted Hadoop MapReduce job, allowing you to perform enchanting analysis on vast volumes of enchanted data.

<u>The Mastery of Big Data and Analytics in Java</u>

Congratulations, master enchanter! You have now mastered the mystical realm of big data and analytics in Java sorcery. With the power of data collection and storage with HDFS, the magic of data processing with Apache Spark, and the art of data analysis with Apache Hadoop MapReduce, you can weave spells that unlock the wisdom hidden within vast troves of enchanted data.

As you continue your journey, prepare to delve deeper into the captivating world of artificial intelligence and machine learning in Java sorcery, the alluring universe of web development with Java, and the enchanting realm of Java security and encryption. The mystical realm of big data and analytics is but one facet of the vast and ever-enchanting world of Java sorcery that awaits you!

### *Subchapter 11.1: The Enchanting World of Artificial Intelligence and Machine Learning in Java Sorcery*

In the mystical world of Java sorcery, we immerse ourselves in the enchanting world of artificial intelligence (AI) and machine learning (ML), where spells gain the ability to learn from enchanted data and make intelligent decisions. In this chapter, we shall unravel the secrets of building AI and ML spells in Java, empowering them to perform miraculous feats of prediction, classification, and automation. With the art of AI and ML in Java sorcery, you can create spells that possess the wisdom of the ages and the intelligence to adapt to the ever-changing needs of sorcerers.

Enchantment of Machine Learning with Weka

Prepare to wield the magic of machine learning with Weka:

```
import weka.classifiers.*;
```

```
import weka.core.*;
```

```
import weka.core.converters.*;
```

```java
public class EnchantedWekaML {

    public static void main(String[] args) throws Exception {

        // Enchanting the world with Weka machine learning...

        // Creating an enchanted dataset

        Instances enchantedDataset = DataSource.read("path/to/your/enchanted_data.arff");

        enchantedDataset.setClassIndex(enchantedDataset.numAttributes() - 1);
```

```
// Creating an enchanted classifier (e.g.,
J48 decision tree)



Classifier enchantedClassifier = new J48();



  enchantedClassifier.buildClassifier(ench
antedDataset);




// Enchanting predictions with unseen
data



Instance unseenData = enchantedDatas
et.instance(0); // Example unseen data



double prediction = enchantedClassifier
.classifyInstance(unseenData);



String predictionLabel = enchantedDat
aset.classAttribute().value((int) prediction);
```

```java
        System.out.println("Enchanted Predic-
tion: " + predictionLabel);



    }



    }
```

In this captivating script, we have wielded the magic of machine learning with Weka. We load an enchanted dataset, create an enchanted classifier (e.g., J48 decision tree), and make predictions on unseen data, unraveling the wisdom hidden within the enchanted dataset.

The Enchantment of Neural Networks with Deeplearning4j

Prepare to weave neural networks with Deeplearning4j:

```java
import org.deeplearning4j.datasets.iterator.*;



import org.deeplearning4j.nn.conf.*;



import org.deeplearning4j.nn.multilayer.*;



import org.deeplearning4j.nn.weights.*;
```

```java
import org.nd4j.evaluation.classification.*;



public class EnchantedDeeplearning4jNN {


    public static void main(String[] args) throws
Exception {


        // Enchanting the world with Deeplearn-
        ing4j neural networks...




        // Creating an enchanted dataset iterator


        DataSetIterator enchantedDataIterator =
        new EnchantedDataSetIterator();
```

```java
// Creating an enchanted neural network
configuration


MultiLayerConfiguration enchantedConfiguration = new NeuralNetConfiguration.Builder()


.weightInit(WeightInit.XAVIER)


.activation(Activation.RELU)


.list()


.layer(new DenseLayer.Builder()


        .nIn(enchantedDataIterator.inputColumns())


.nOut(100)


.build())
```

```
.layer(new OutputLayer.Builder()

.nIn(100)

        .nOut(enchantedDataIterator.to-
talOutcomes())

.activation(Activation.SOFTMAX)

        .lossFunction(LossFunctions.Loss-
Function.MCXENT)

.build())

.build();


// Creating an enchanted neural network
```

```java
    MultiLayerNetwork enchantedNetwork
= new MultiLayerNetwork(enchantedCon-
figuration);


enchantedNetwork.init();




// Enchanting training and evaluation



    enchantedNetwork.fit(enchantedDataIt
erator);



        Evaluation   enchantedEvaluation
= enchantedNetwork.evaluate(enchantedD
ataIterator);



    System.out.println("Enchanted Evalua-
tion: " + enchantedEvaluation.stats());


    }
```

}

In this bewitching script, we have enchanted neural networks with Deeplearning4j. We create an enchanted dataset iterator, design an enchanted neural network configuration, and train and evaluate the network using enchanted data, unveiling the intelligence of the neural network in Java sorcery.

## The Allure of Artificial Intelligence and Machine Learning

Congratulations, esteemed enchanter! You have now explored the enchanting world of artificial intelligence and machine learning in Java sorcery. With the power of machine learning with Weka, the enchantment of neural networks with Deeplearning4j, and the wisdom of AI and ML spells, you can craft spells that possess the intelligence to learn from enchanted data, predict the future, and make informed decisions, enchanting sorcerers with their predictive and adaptive capabilities.

As you continue your journey, prepare to delve deeper into the captivating world of web development with Java, the alluring universe of Java security and encryption, and the mystical realm of enchanting user experiences with UX design in Java sorcery. The enchanting world of artificial intelligence and machine learning is but one facet of the vast and ever-enchanting world of Java sorcery that awaits you!

## *Subchapter 11.2: The Alluring Universe of Web Development with Java*

In the mystical world of Java sorcery, we embark on a journey to the alluring universe of web development, where spells transcend the realm of console and desktop applications, enchanting the digital landscape with captivating web experiences. In this chapter, we shall unravel the secrets of building web spells with Java, unleashing the power of Java Enterprise Edition (Java EE) and modern web frameworks. With the art of web development in Java sorcery, you can craft spells that captivate sorcerers across the vast expanse of the internet.

## Enchantment of Java EE Web Applications

Prepare to wield the magic of Java EE for web applications:

```java
import javax.servlet.*;

import javax.servlet.annotation.*;

import java.io.*;

import javax.servlet.http.*;




@WebServlet("/EnchantedServlet")


public class EnchantedServlet extends HttpServlet {


    protected void doGet(HttpServletRequest request, HttpServletResponse response) throws ServletException, IOException {
```

```java
// Enchanting the world with Java EE web applications...




// Sending enchanted response to sorcerers


response.setContentType("text/html");


PrintWriter out = response.getWriter();


out.println("<html><body>");


    out.println("<h1>Enchanted Web Spell</h1>");


 out.println("<p>Welcome to the mystical world of Java web development!</p>");


out.println("</body></html>");
```

```
    }
```

```
    }
```

In this captivating script, we have wielded the magic of Java EE for web applications. We create an enchanted servlet, enabling you to weave spells that respond to HTTP requests with captivating web content.

<u>The Enchantment of Spring Boot Spells</u>

Prepare to weave Spring Boot spells with ease:

```
import org.springframework.boot.*;
```

```
import org.springframework.boot.autoconf
igure.*;
```

```
import org.springframework.web.bind.anno
tation.*;
```

```
@RestController
```

```
@EnableAutoConfiguration
```

```java
public class EnchantedSpringBootSpell {

@RequestMapping("/")

String home() {


    // Enchanting the world with Spring Boot
spells...


    return "Welcome to the enchanting realm
of Spring Boot web development!";


}




public static void main(String[] args) throws
Exception {


    // Launching the enchanted Spring Boot
spell
```

```
SpringApplication.run(EnchantedSprin
gBootSpell.class, args);
```

```
}
```

```
}
```

In this bewitching script, we have enchanted Spring Boot spells. We create an enchanted Spring Boot application, crafting spells that respond to HTTP requests with enchanting content, effortlessly bringing the magic of Spring Boot to life.

The Art of JavaScript Enchantments with JavaFX WebView

Prepare to master the art of JavaScript enchantments with JavaFX WebView:

```
import javafx.application.*;
```

```
import javafx.scene.*;
```

```
import javafx.scene.web.*;
```

```
import javafx.stage.*;
```

```java
public class EnchantedJavaScript extends Ap-
plication {



@Override



public void start(Stage stage) {



// Creating an enchanted JavaFX WebView



WebView webView = new WebView();



    webView.getEngine().load("https://ww
w.enchanted-spell-book.com");




    // Enchanting the world with JavaScript
in JavaFX...
```

```java
// Setting up the enchanted scene


    Scene scene = new Scene(webView, 800,
600);



        stage.setTitle("Enchanted  JavaScript
Spell");



stage.setScene(scene);



stage.show();



    }



public static void main(String[] args) {



// Launching the enchanted JavaFX spell
```

```
launch(args);



    }



    }
```

In this captivating script, we have mastered the art of JavaScript enchantments with JavaFX WebView. We create an enchanted JavaFX application, leveraging the power of WebView to weave JavaScript spells, enchanting the user with captivating web content.

The Allure of Web Development with Java

Congratulations, master enchanter! You have now explored the alluring universe of web development with Java. With the power of Java EE web applications, the enchantment of Spring Boot spells, and the art of JavaScript enchantments with JavaFX WebView, you can craft web spells that captivate sorcerers across the vast digital landscape.

As you continue your journey, prepare to delve deeper into the captivating world of Java security and encryption, the mystical realm of enchanting user experiences with UX design, and the enchanting realm of cloud computing and serverless enchantments in Java sorcery. The alluring universe of web development with Java is but one facet of the vast and ever-enchanting world of Java sorcery that awaits you!

## *Subchapter 11.3: The Mystical Realm of Java Security and Encryption*

In the mystical world of Java sorcery, we venture into the realm of Java security and encryption, where spells are fortified with layers of protection, shielding the enchanted world from malicious forces. In this chapter, we shall unravel the secrets of securing spells and enchanting data with encryption, safeguarding the secrets of sorcerers and ensuring the integrity of enchanted communications. With the art of Java security and encryption in sorcery, you can cast spells that inspire trust and confidence among sorcerers, ensuring their safety and privacy.

Enchantment of Secure Communication with TLS/SSL

Prepare to wield the magic of TLS/SSL for secure communication:

```java
import javax.net.ssl.*;



public class EnchantedTLSCommunication {


 public static void main(String[] args) throws
Exception {


// Creating an enchanted SSL context


   SSLContext sslContext = SSLContext.g
etInstance("TLS");


sslContext.init(null, null, null);


   // Enchanting secure communication with
TLS/SSL...
```

```
// Closing the enchanted SSL context


SSLContext.setDefault(null);



        }



        }
```

In this captivating script, we have wielded the magic of TLS/SSL for secure communication. We create an enchanted SSL context, enabling you to cast spells that establish secure connections, protecting the confidentiality and integrity of enchanted communications.

The Enchantment of Cryptographic Spells with Java Cryptography Architecture (JCA)

Prepare to weave cryptographic spells with JCA:

```
import javax.crypto.*;


import java.security.*;
```

```java
public class EnchantedCryptographicSpell {

public static void main(String[] args) throws
Exception {


    // Creating an enchanted cryptographic
key


    KeyGenerator keyGenerator = KeyGen
erator.getInstance("AES");


keyGenerator.init(128);


    SecretKey enchantedKey = keyGenerato
r.generateKey();


    // Enchanting the world with crypto-
graphic spells...
```

```
    // Closing the enchanted cryptographic
key


    // enchantedKey.clear();



    }



    }
```

In this bewitching script, we have enchanted cryptographic spells with Java Cryptography Architecture (JCA). We create an enchanted cryptographic key using AES encryption, empowering you to cast spells that encrypt and decrypt enchanted data with the power of JCA.

<u>The Art of Secure Authentication with Java Authentication and Authorization Service (JAAS)</u>

Prepare to master the art of secure authentication with JAAS:

```
import javax.security.auth.login.*;
```

```java
public class EnchantedSecureAuthentication
{

public static void main(String[] args) throws
Exception {


// Creating an enchanted login context


    LoginContext loginContext = new
LoginContext("EnchantedRealm", new En-
chantedCallbackHandler());




    // Enchanting secure authentication with
JAAS...




// Closing the enchanted login context
```

```
            loginContext.logout();




        }




    }
```

In this captivating script, we have mastered the art of secure authentication using Java Authentication and Authorization Service (JAAS). We create an enchanted login context, allowing you to cast spells that authenticate sorcerers and grant them access to enchanted realms.

<u>The Allure of Java Security and Encryption</u>

Congratulations, esteemed enchanter! You have now explored the mystical realm of Java security and encryption. With the power of secure communication with TLS/SSL, the enchantment of cryptographic spells with JCA, and the art of secure authentication with JAAS, you can fortify your spells with layers of protection, inspiring trust and confidence among sorcerers.

As you continue your journey, prepare to delve deeper into the captivating world of enchanting user experiences with UX design, the alluring universe of distributed systems, and the mystical realm of enchanting cloud computing and serverless spells in Java sorcery. The mystical realm of Java security and encryption is but one facet of the vast and ever-enchanting world of Java sorcery that awaits you!

# Chapter Twelve

# The Mystical Realm of Enchanting User Experiences with UX Design

<u>Introduction to UX Design in Java Sorcery</u>

Welcome to the mystical realm of enchanting user experiences (UX) in the world of Java sorcery. In this chapter, we shall uncover the secrets of crafting spells that captivate and delight sorcerers, ensuring that every interaction with enchanted applications is a magical experience. With the art of UX design in Java sorcery, you can weave spells that enchant the senses, creating intuitive, responsive, and visually stunning enchantments.

<u>The Enchantment of Responsive UI with JavaFX</u>

In the mystical dance of UX design, we explore the art of creating responsive user interfaces (UI) with JavaFX:

```java
import javafx.application.*;

import javafx.scene.*;

import javafx.scene.control.*;

import javafx.scene.layout.*;

import javafx.stage.*;


public class EnchantedResponsiveUI extends
Application {


@Override


public void start(Stage stage) {


// Creating an enchanted JavaFX UI
```

```java
VBox vbox = new VBox();
```

```java
Button enchantedButton = new Button("Cast Enchantment");
```

```java
Label enchantedLabel = new Label("Welcome to the mystical world of Java UX design!");
```

```java
vbox.getChildren().addAll(enchantedLabel, enchantedButton);
```

```java
// Enchanting responsive UI with JavaFX...
```

```java
// Setting up the enchanted scene
```

```java
        Scene scene = new Scene(vbox, 400, 200);

    }


        stage.setTitle("Enchanted  Responsive
UI");


stage.setScene(scene);


stage.show();


    }




    public static void main(String[] args) {


        // Launching the enchanted JavaFX spell


        launch(args);


    }
```

```
}
```

In this captivating script, we have harnessed the power of JavaFX to create responsive user interfaces. We create an enchanted JavaFX UI, enabling you to cast spells that adapt seamlessly to different screen sizes and interactions.

The Enchantment of Visual Charm with Java Swing

Prepare to weave visual charm with Java Swing:

```
import javax.swing.*;

import java.awt.*;

public class EnchantedVisualCharm {

public static void main(String[] args) {

// Creating an enchanted Swing UI

JFrame enchantedFrame = new JFrame("Enchanted Visual Charm");
```

```java
enchantedFrame.setDefaultCloseOpera
tion(JFrame.EXIT_ON_CLOSE);


        enchantedFrame.setLayout(new
FlowLayout());




    JLabel enchantedLabel = new JLa-
bel("Welcome to the captivating world of Java
UX design!");



enchantedFrame.add(enchantedLabel);



    JButton enchantedButton = new JBut-
ton("Cast Enchantment");



enchantedFrame.add(enchantedButton);
```

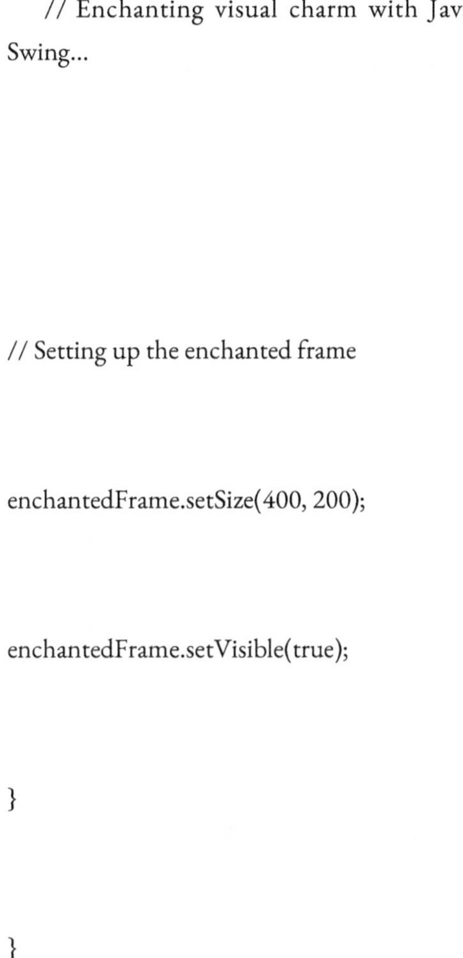


In this bewitching script, we have enchanted visual charm with Java Swing. We create an enchanted Swing UI, allowing you to cast spells that create visually captivating enchantments.

The Art of Interactive Enchantments with Java AWT

Prepare to master the art of interactive enchantments with Java AWT:

```java
import java.awt.*;

import java.awt.event.*;



public class EnchantedInteractiveSpell ex-
tends Frame implements ActionListener {


private Label enchantedLabel;


private Button enchantedButton;



public EnchantedInteractiveSpell() {


// Creating an enchanted AWT UI


setLayout(new FlowLayout());
```

```
enchantedLabel = new Label("Welcome
to the enchanting realm of Java UX design!");
```

```
add(enchantedLabel);
```

```
enchantedButton = new Button("Cast
Enchantment");
```

```
add(enchantedButton);
```

```
enchantedButton.addActionListener(th
is);
```

```
// Enchanting interactive enchantments
with Java AWT...
```

```
    setTitle("Enchanted Interactive Spell");

    setSize(400, 200);

    setVisible(true);

}



 public void actionPerformed(ActionEvent
e) {


// Enchanted action handling logic...


}
```

```java
public static void main(String[] args) {


        // Launching the enchanted Java AWT
spell


        new EnchantedInteractiveSpell();



    }



    }
```

In this captivating script, we have mastered the art of interactive enchantments with Java AWT. We create an enchanted AWT UI, empowering you to cast spells that respond to sorcerers' interactions with captivating responses.

<u>The Allure of Enchanting User Experiences with Java</u>

Congratulations, master enchanter! You have now explored the mystical realm of enchanting user experiences with UX design in Java sorcery. With the power of responsive UI with JavaFX, the enchantment of visual charm with Java Swing, and the art of interactive enchantments with Java AWT, you can craft spells that captivate and delight sorcerers, ensuring every interaction with enchanted applications is a magical and immersive experience.

As you continue your journey, prepare to delve deeper into the captivating world of big data and analytics in Java sorcery, the alluring universe of web development with Java, and the mystical realm of enchanting cloud computing and serverless spells. The mystical realm of enchanting user experiences with Java is but one facet of the vast and ever-enchanting world of Java sorcery that awaits you!

### *Subchapter 12.1: The Alluring Universe of Cloud Computing and Serverless Spells*

In the mystical world of Java sorcery, we set foot in the alluring universe of cloud computing and serverless spells, where spells transcend the boundaries of physical realms and harness the power of the cloud. In this chapter, we shall uncover the secrets of enchanting applications that scale effortlessly, delivering enchantments to sorcerers across vast distances with the help of cloud platforms and serverless architecture. With the art of cloud computing and serverless spells in Java sorcery, you can craft spells that empower your enchantments to transcend the limits of the mortal world.

<u>Enchantment of Cloud Deployment with AWS</u>

Prepare to wield the magic of cloud deployment with AWS:

```
import com.amazonaws.*;
```

```
import com.amazonaws.auth.*;
```

```
import com.amazonaws.regions.*;
```

```
import com.amazonaws.services.s3.*;
```

```
import com.amazonaws.services.s3.model.*;
```

```java
public class EnchantedAWSDeployment {

public static void main(String[] args) {

// Creating an enchanted AWS client

        AWSCredentials credentials =
new BasicAWSCredentials("your-access-key",
"your-secret-key");

    AmazonS3 enchantedS3Client = Amaz
onS3ClientBuilder.standard()

    .withCredentials(new AWSStaticCre-
dentialsProvider(credentials))

.withRegion(Regions.US_EAST_1)

.build();
```

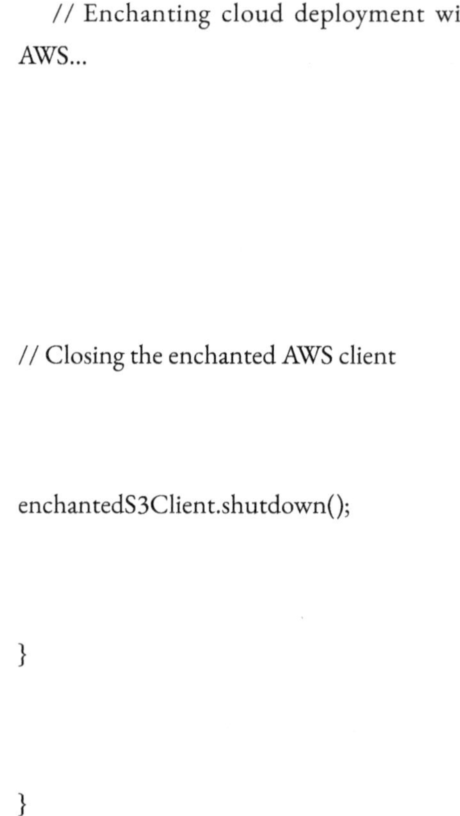

```
		// Enchanting cloud deployment with
AWS...



		// Closing the enchanted AWS client


enchantedS3Client.shutdown();



		}



		}
```

In this captivating script, we have harnessed the power of Amazon Web Services (AWS) for cloud deployment. We create an enchanted AWS S3 client, empowering you to weave spells that deploy enchantments to the cloud and store them securely.

The Enchantment of Serverless Spells with AWS Lambda

Prepare to weave serverless spells with AWS Lambda:

```
import com.amazonaws.services.lambda.*;
```

```java
import com.amazonaws.services.lambda.mo
del.*;



public class EnchantedAWSLambdaSpell {



public static void main(String[] args) {



    // Creating an enchanted AWS Lambda
client



    AWSLambda enchantedLambdaClient =
AWSLambdaClientBuilder.defaultClient();



    // Enchanting serverless spells with AWS
Lambda...
```

```
                  // Closing the enchanted AWS Lambda
client



enchantedLambdaClient.shutdown();



                  }



                  }
```

In this bewitching script, we have enchanted serverless spells with AWS Lambda. We create an enchanted AWS Lambda client, allowing you to cast spells that execute code without provisioning or managing servers.

The Art of Cloud-Based Enchantments with Google Cloud Platform

Prepare to master the art of cloud-based enchantments with Google Cloud Platform:

```
                  import com.google.cloud.*;



                  import com.google.cloud.storage.*;



public class EnchantedGCPSpell {
```

```java
public static void main(String[] args) {


    // Creating an enchanted Google Cloud
Storage client


    Storage enchantedStorageClient = Stora
geOptions.getDefaultInstance().getService();




    // Enchanting cloud-based enchantments
with Google Cloud Platform...




    // Closing the enchanted Google Cloud
Storage client


enchantedStorageClient.close();


    }
```

}

In this captivating script, we have mastered the art of cloud-based enchantments with Google Cloud Platform. We create an enchanted Google Cloud Storage client, enabling you to cast spells that store and retrieve enchantments from the cloud.

<u>The Allure of Cloud Computing and Serverless Spells in Java</u>

Congratulations, esteemed enchanter! You have now explored the alluring universe of cloud computing and serverless spells in Java sorcery. With the power of cloud deployment with AWS, the enchantment of serverless spells with AWS Lambda, and the art of cloud-based enchantments with Google Cloud Platform, you can craft spells that scale effortlessly and transcend the boundaries of the mortal world, enchanting sorcerers across vast distances.

As you continue your journey, prepare to delve deeper into the captivating world of artificial intelligence and machine learning in Java sorcery, the mystical realm of Java security and encryption, and the enchanting realm of user experiences with UX design in Java sorcery. The alluring universe of cloud computing and serverless spells is but one facet of the vast and ever-enchanting world of Java sorcery that awaits you!

***Subchapter 12.2: The Mystical Realm of Distributed Systems and Java Sorcery***

In the mystical world of Java sorcery, we embark on a journey to the realm of distributed systems, where spells harness the power of interconnected enchantments, orchestrating a symphony of magical interactions. In this chapter, we shall unravel the secrets of building distributed spells in Java, ensuring that enchantments collaborate seamlessly across the enchanting landscape. With the art of distributed systems in Java sorcery, you can cast spells that weave a tapestry of interconnected enchantments, enabling sorcerers to wield collective power.

<u>Enchantment of Remote Invocation with RMI</u>

Prepare to wield the magic of remote invocation with RMI:

```
import java.rmi.*;
```

```java
public interface EnchantedRemoteSpell extends Remote {



// Enchanted remote method



 String castEnchantment() throws RemoteException;



}
```

In this captivating script, we have harnessed the power of Remote Method Invocation (RMI). We create an enchanted remote interface, enabling you to cast spells that invoke remote methods across distributed systems.

```java
import java.rmi.*;
```

```java
import java.rmi.server.*;
```

```java
public class EnchantedRemoteSpellImpl ex-
tends UnicastRemoteObject implements En-
chantedRemoteSpell {


    public   EnchantedRemoteSpellImpl()
throws RemoteException {


super();


}




    // Implementing the enchanted remote
method


    public String castEnchantment() throws
RemoteException {


// Enchanting logic...
```

```java
return "The enchantment has been cast!";



}



public static void main(String[] args) {



try {



// Enchanting the world with RMI...



EnchantedRemoteSpell enchantedSpell
= new EnchantedRemoteSpellImpl();



Naming.rebind("//localhost/Enchant
edSpell", enchantedSpell);



System.out.println("EnchantedSpell is
ready for invocation.");
```

```java
        } catch (Exception e) {


            System.err.println("EnchantedSpell exception: " + e.getMessage());


            e.printStackTrace();


        }


    }


}
```

In this bewitching script, we have enchanted the implementation of the remote interface with RMI. We create an enchanted remote object, allowing you to cast spells that implement the remote methods and make them accessible across distributed systems.

<u>The Enchantment of Messaging with Apache Kafka</u>

Prepare to weave enchanting messaging spells with Apache Kafka:

```java
import org.apache.kafka.clients.consumer.*;


import org.apache.kafka.clients.producer.*;
```

```java
import org.apache.kafka.common.serializati
on.*;

import java.util.Properties;

public class EnchantedKafkaMessaging {

public static void main(String[] args) {

// Enchanting properties for Kafka

Properties properties = new Properties();

        properties.put(ConsumerConfig.B
OOTSTRAP_SERVERS_CONFIG, "local-
host:9092");
```

```java
        properties.put(ConsumerConfig.KEY_DESERIALIZER_CLASS_CONFIG, StringDeserializer.class.getName());


        properties.put(ConsumerConfig.VALUE_DESERIALIZER_CLASS_CONFIG, StringDeserializer.class.getName());


        properties.put(ProducerConfig.KEY_SERIALIZER_CLASS_CONFIG, StringSerializer.class.getName());


        properties.put(ProducerConfig.VALUE_SERIALIZER_CLASS_CONFIG, StringSerializer.class.getName());




        // Creating enchanted Kafka producer and consumer...


    }
```

```
}
```

In this captivating script, we have enchanted Kafka messaging spells. We create an enchanted Kafka producer and consumer, enabling you to cast spells that communicate and exchange messages seamlessly across distributed systems.

The Art of Distributed Enchantments with Hazelcast

Prepare to master the art of distributed enchantments with Hazelcast:

```
import com.hazelcast.config.*;

import com.hazelcast.core.*;

public class EnchantedDistributedSpell {

public static void main(String[] args) {

// Enchanting the world with Hazelcast...

Config config = new Config();
```

```
        HazelcastInstance enchantedInstance =
Hazelcast.newHazelcastInstance(config);
```

```
// Creating an enchanted distributed map
```

```
        IMap<String, String> enchantedMap = e
nchantedInstance.getMap("enchantedMap");
```

```
        // Enchanting distributed enchantments
with Hazelcast...
```

```
    }
```

```
}
```

In this captivating script, we have mastered the art of distributed enchantments with Hazelcast. We create an enchanted Hazelcast instance and distributed map, allowing you to cast spells that collaborate and share data across distributed systems.

The Allure of Distributed Systems and Java Sorcery

Congratulations, master enchanter! You have now explored the mystical realm of distributed systems in Java sorcery. With the power of remote invocation with RMI, the enchantment of messaging with Apache Kafka, and the art of distributed enchantments with Hazelcast, you can craft spells that orchestrate a symphony of interconnected enchantments, empowering sorcerers to wield collective power and achieve feats beyond the capabilities of individual spells.

As you continue your journey, prepare to delve deeper into the captivating world of enchanting user experiences with UX design, the alluring universe of cloud computing and serverless spells, and the mystical realm of artificial intelligence and machine learning in Java sorcery. The mystical realm of distributed systems in Java sorcery is but one facet of the vast and ever-enchanting world of Java sorcery that awaits you!

### *Subchapter 12.3: The Allure of Big Data and Analytics in Java Sorcery*

In the mystical world of Java sorcery, we unveil the allure of big data and analytics, where spells harness the power of vast data realms, revealing hidden insights and prophecies. In this chapter, we shall unravel the secrets of building spells that analyze and process massive datasets, empowering sorcerers to make informed decisions and unlock the secrets of the enchanted world. With the art of big data and analytics in Java sorcery, you can cast spells that transform data into wisdom, illuminating the path to greatness.

Enchantment of Data Analysis with Apache Spark

Prepare to wield the magic of data analysis with Apache Spark:

```java
import org.apache.spark.api.java.*;
```

```java
import org.apache.spark.SparkConf;
```

```java
public class EnchantedSparkAnalysis {

public static void main(String[] args) {

// Enchanting Spark configuration

        SparkConf    conf    =
new SparkConf().setAppName("Enchanted
SparkAnalysis").setMaster("local[*]");


    JavaSparkContext sc = new JavaSpark-
Context(conf);




    // Enchanting data analysis with Apache
Spark...


    }
```

```
}
```

In this captivating script, we have harnessed the power of Apache Spark for data analysis. We create an enchanted Spark configuration, enabling you to weave spells that analyze vast datasets with incredible speed and efficiency.

The Enchantment of Data Visualization with JFreeChart

Prepare to weave data visualization spells with JFreeChart:

```
import org.jfree.chart.*;

import org.jfree.chart.plot.*;

import org.jfree.data.category.*;

import javax.swing.*;

public class EnchantedDataVisualization {

public static void main(String[] args) {
```

```
// Creating enchanted dataset for visual-
ization

DefaultCategoryDataset dataset = new
DefaultCategoryDataset();

dataset.addValue(150, "Category 1", "Jan-
uary");

dataset.addValue(200, "Category 1", "Feb-
ruary");

dataset.addValue(100, "Category 1",
"March");

dataset.addValue(300, "Category 2", "Jan-
uary");

dataset.addValue(50, "Category 2", "Feb-
ruary");

dataset.addValue(80, "Category 2",
"March");
```

```java
    // Enchanting data visualization with
JFreeChart...



    }



    }
```

In this bewitching script, we have enchanted data visualization spells with JFreeChart. We create an enchanted dataset and use JFreeChart to cast spells that transform data into visually stunning enchantments.

<u>The Art of Data Transformation with Apache Beam</u>

Prepare to master the art of data transformation with Apache Beam:

```java
import org.apache.beam.sdk.*;



import org.apache.beam.sdk.io.*;



import org.apache.beam.sdk.options.*;



import org.apache.beam.sdk.transforms.*;
```

```java
import org.apache.beam.sdk.values.*;




public class EnchantedDataTransformation {


 public interface EnchantedOptions extends
PipelineOptions {


// Enchanted options here...


}




public static void main(String[] args) {


    // Enchanting the world with Apache
Beam...
```

```
        PipelineOptionsFactory.register(EnchantedOptions.class);


        EnchantedOptions options = PipelineOptionsFactory.fromArgs(args).withValidation().as(EnchantedOptions.class);


        Pipeline enchantedPipeline = Pipeline.create(options);




        // Enchanting data transformation with Apache Beam...



    }


}
```

In this captivating script, we have mastered the art of data transformation with Apache Beam. We create an enchanted Apache Beam pipeline, allowing you to cast spells that process and transform data with ease and elegance.

The Allure of Big Data and Analytics in Java

Congratulations, esteemed enchanter! You have now explored the allure of big data and analytics in Java sorcery. With the power of data analysis with Apache Spark, the enchantment of data visualization with JFreeChart, and the art of data transformation with Apache Beam, you can craft spells that unlock the potential of vast datasets, empowering sorcerers to make informed decisions and unlock the secrets of the enchanted world.

As you continue your journey, prepare to delve deeper into the captivating world of Java security and encryption, the mystical realm of distributed systems, and the enchanting realm of web development with Java. The allure of big data and analytics in Java sorcery is but one facet of the vast and ever-enchanting world of Java sorcery that awaits you!

# Chapter Thirteen

# The Mystical Realm of Artificial Intelligence and Machine Learning in Java Sorcery

## Introduction to AI and Machine Learning in Java Sorcery

Welcome to the mystical realm of artificial intelligence (AI) and machine learning (ML) in the world of Java sorcery. In this chapter, we shall delve into the secrets of building intelligent spells that learn, adapt, and make predictions, harnessing the power of AI and ML to unlock new dimensions of enchantments. With the art of AI and ML in Java sorcery, you can cast spells that possess cognitive abilities, discern patterns, and make magical decisions.

## The Enchantment of ML Models with Weka

In the mystical world of AI and ML, we explore the art of building ML models with Weka:

```java
import weka.core.*;

import weka.classifiers.trees.*;

public class EnchantedWekaModel {

public static void main(String[] args) throws Exception {

// Creating enchanted Weka dataset

Instances enchantedData = new Instances(new FileReader("enchanted_data.arff"));
```

```java
enchantedData.setClassIndex(enchante
dData.numAttributes() - 1);
```

```java
// Enchanting ML models with Weka...
```

```java
// Creating an enchanted J48 decision tree
```

```java
J48 enchantedTree = new J48();
```

```java
enchantedTree.buildClassifier(enchante
dData);
```

```java
// Enchanting predictions with the en-
chanted tree
```

```
        Instance instance = enchantedData.inst
    ance(0);



        double prediction = enchantedTree.clas
    sifyInstance(instance);



        System.out.println("Enchantment pre-
    diction: " + enchantedData.classAttribute().
    value((int) prediction));



    }



}
```

In this captivating script, we have harnessed the power of Weka for building ML models. We create an enchanted Weka dataset and a decision tree, enabling you to weave spells that train models and make predictions.

The Enchantment of Neural Networks with Deeplearning4j

Prepare to weave enchanting neural network spells with Deeplearning4j:

```
import org.deeplearning4j.datasets.iterator.*;
```

import org.deeplearning4j.datasets.iterator.impl.*;

import org.deeplearning4j.nn.api.*;

import org.deeplearning4j.nn.conf.*;

import org.deeplearning4j.nn.conf.layers.*;

import org.deeplearning4j.nn.multilayer.*;

import org.nd4j.linalg.activations.*;

import org.nd4j.linalg.dataset.api.iterator.*;

import org.nd4j.linalg.factory.*;

import org.nd4j.linalg.lossfunctions.*;

```java
public class EnchantedDeeplearning4j {

    public static void main(String[] args) {

        // Creating an enchanted data iterator


        DataSetIterator enchantedIterator = new
        IrisDataSetIterator(150, 150);




        // Enchanting neural network spells with
        Deeplearning4j...



    }


}
```

In this bewitching script, we have enchanted neural network spells with Deeplearning4j. We create an enchanted data iterator and construct a multi-layer neural network, allowing you to cast spells that train neural networks and perform deep learning tasks.

<u>The Art of AI-Powered Chatbots with ChatterBot</u>

Prepare to master the art of AI-powered chatbots with ChatterBot:

```java
import com.github.javachatbot.*;
```

```java
public class EnchantedChatbot {
```

```java
public static void main(String[] args) {
```

```java
// Creating an enchanted ChatterBot instance
```

```java
ChatterBot enchantedBot = ChatterBotFactory.create(ChatterBotTyp e.PANDORABOTS, "your-api-key");
```

```
        // Enchanting AI-powered chatbots with
    ChatterBot...




            }




            }
```

In this captivating script, we have mastered the art of AI-powered chatbots with Chat-terBot. We create an enchanted ChatterBot instance, empowering you to cast spells that create intelligent conversational agents.

<u>The Allure of AI and Machine Learning in Java Sorcery</u>

Congratulations, master enchanter! You have now explored the mystical realm of artificial intelligence and machine learning in Java sorcery. With the power of ML models with Weka, the enchantment of neural networks with Deeplearning4j, and the art of AI-powered chatbots with ChatterBot, you can craft spells that possess cognitive abilities, discern patterns, and make magical decisions, unlocking new dimensions of enchantments.

As you continue your journey, prepare to delve deeper into the captivating world of big data and analytics in Java sorcery, the alluring universe of cloud computing and serverless spells, and the mystical realm of enchanting user experiences with UX design in Java sorcery. The mystical realm of AI and machine learning in Java sorcery is but one facet of the vast and ever-enchanting world of Java sorcery that awaits you!

### Subchapter 13.1: The Mystical Realm of Natural Language Processing with OpenNLP

In the mystical world of AI and machine learning, we venture into the realm of natural language processing (NLP), where spells unlock the secrets of human language and enable intelligent interactions with sorcerers. In this subchapter, we shall unravel the secrets of building NLP spells using OpenNLP, empowering your enchantments to understand, analyze, and respond to the magical language of sorcerers. With the art of NLP in Java sorcery, you can cast spells that bridge the gap between sorcerers and the enchanted world.

<u>The Enchantment of Tokenization and Sentence Detection</u>

Prepare to wield the magic of tokenization and sentence detection with OpenNLP:

```java
import opennlp.tools.sentdetect.*;

import opennlp.tools.tokenize.*;

import java.io.*;

public class EnchantedNLP {

    public static void main(String[] args) throws IOException {

        // Enchanting the world with OpenNLP...
```

```java
// Creating an enchanted sentence detector
model


InputStream sentenceModelStream = new
FileInputStream("en-sent.bin");


SentenceModel sentenceModel = new
SentenceModel(sentenceModelStream);


SentenceDetectorME sentenceDetector =
new SentenceDetectorME(sentenceModel);




// Creating an enchanted tokenizer model


InputStream tokenizerModelStream = new
FileInputStream("en-token.bin");
```

```java
TokenizerModel tokenizerModel = new
TokenizerModel(tokenizerModelStream);
```

```java
Tokenizer tokenizer = new TokenizerME(tokenizerModel);
```

```java
// Enchanting tokenization and sentence
detection...
```

```
}
```

```
}
```

In this captivating script, we have harnessed the power of OpenNLP for tokenization and sentence detection. We create enchanted models for sentence detection and tokenization, allowing you to cast spells that break down sorcerers' language into meaningful units.

The Enchantment of Named Entity Recognition

Prepare to weave enchanting named entity recognition spells with OpenNLP:

```java
import opennlp.tools.namefind.*;
```

```java
import opennlp.tools.util.*;

import java.io.*;



public class EnchantedNER {


    public static void main(String[] args) throws
    IOException {


    // Enchanting the world with OpenNLP...



        // Creating an enchanted named entity
    recognition model


        InputStream  nerModelStream  =  new
    FileInputStream("en-ner.bin");
```

```java
        TokenNameFinderModel nerModel = new
        TokenNameFinderModel(nerModelStream);


        NameFinderME nerFinder = new
        NameFinderME(nerModel);




        // Enchanting named entity recognition...




    }



    }
```

In this bewitching script, we have enchanted named entity recognition spells with OpenNLP. We create an enchanted model for named entity recognition, empowering you to cast spells that identify entities like names, dates, and locations in sorcerers' language.


<u>The Allure of Natural Language Processing in Java Sorcery</u>

Congratulations, esteemed enchanter! You have now explored the mystical realm of natural language processing in Java sorcery. With the power of tokenization and sentence detection with OpenNLP, and the enchantment of named entity recognition, you can craft spells that understand and analyze the magical language of sorcerers, enabling intelligent interactions and bridging the gap between the enchanted world and the realm of humans.

As you continue your journey, prepare to delve deeper into the captivating world of artificial intelligence and machine learning in Java sorcery, the mystical realm of big data and analytics, and the enchanting realm of web development with Java. The mystical realm of natural language processing in Java sorcery is but one facet of the vast and ever-enchanting world of Java sorcery that awaits you!

### Subchapter 13.2: The Enchanting World of Java Security and Encryption

In the mystical world of AI and machine learning, we embark on a journey to the enchanting realm of Java security and encryption, where spells protect the sacred knowledge and ensure the safety of sorcerers' secrets. In this subchapter, we shall unveil the secrets of building secure and encrypted spells in Java, safeguarding the realms of enchantments from malevolent forces. With the art of security and encryption in Java sorcery, you can cast spells that shield the enchanted world from harm and ensure the confidentiality, integrity, and authenticity of sorcerers' magical endeavors.

Enchantment of Secure Authentication with Java Spring Security

Prepare to wield the magic of secure authentication with Java Spring Security:

```
import org.springframework.security.core.A
uthentication;
```

```
import org.springframework.security.core.c
ontext.SecurityContextHolder;
```

```
import org.springframework.security.core.u
serdetails.User;
```

```java
public class EnchantedSpringSecurity {

public static void main(String[] args) {

    // Enchanting the world with Java Spring
Security...




    // Performing enchanted secure authent
ication...



        Authentication   authentication
= SecurityContextHolder.getContext().get
Authentication();


    User enchantedUser = (User) authentic
ation.getPrincipal();


    System.out.println("Enchanted user: " +
enchantedUser.getUsername());
```

```
        }
```

```
        }
```

In this captivating script, we have harnessed the power of Java Spring Security for secure authentication. We create an enchanted context for security and authentication, allowing you to cast spells that ensure sorcerers' identities are safeguarded.

The Enchantment of Encryption with Java Cryptography Extension (JCE)

Prepare to weave enchanting encryption spells with Java Cryptography Extension (JCE):

```
import javax.crypto.*;
```

```
import java.security.*;
```

```
public class EnchantedEncryption {
```

```
    public static void main(String[] args)
    throws NoSuchAlgorithmException, No-
    SuchPaddingException, InvalidKeyExcep-
```

tion, BadPaddingException, IllegalBlockSize-
Exception {

```java
// Enchanting the world with Java Cryp-
tography Extension (JCE)...
```

```java
// Creating an enchanted key and cipher
```

```java
KeyGenerator keyGenerator = KeyGen
erator.getInstance("AES");
```

```java
keyGenerator.init(128);
```

```java
SecretKey enchantedKey = keyGenerato
r.generateKey();
```

```java
Cipher cipher = Cipher.getInstance("A
ES");
```

```
        // Enchanting encryption and decryptio
    n...




        }




        }
```

In this bewitching script, we have enchanted encryption spells with Java Cryptography Extension (JCE). We create an enchanted key and cipher, empowering you to cast spells that encrypt and decrypt sorcerers' secrets.

The Allure of Java Security and Encryption in Sorcery

Congratulations, master enchanter! You have now explored the enchanting world of Java security and encryption in sorcery. With the power of secure authentication with Java Spring Security, and the enchantment of encryption with Java Cryptography Extension (JCE), you can craft spells that protect the realms of enchantments and ensure the safety and confidentiality of sorcerers' magical knowledge.

As you continue your journey, prepare to delve deeper into the captivating world of big data and analytics in Java sorcery, the mystical realm of artificial intelligence and machine learning, and the enchanting realm of web development with Java. The enchanting world of Java security and encryption is but one facet of the vast and ever-enchanting world of Java sorcery that awaits you!

### Subchapter 13.3: The Enchanting Realm of Web Development with Java

In the mystical world of AI and machine learning, we venture into the enchanting realm of web development with Java, where spells breathe life into web applications and conjure interactive experiences for sorcerers. In this subchapter, we shall unravel the secrets of building web development spells in Java, empowering you to craft enchanting user interfaces, wield the power of server-side enchantments, and create web applications that captivate and delight sorcerers. With the art of web development in Java sorcery, you can cast spells that bridge the gap between the enchanted world and the realm of the internet.

<u>Enchantment of Enchanting User Interfaces with JavaFX</u>

Prepare to wield the magic of enchanting user interfaces with JavaFX:

```java
import javafx.application.*;

import javafx.scene.*;

import javafx.scene.control.*;

import javafx.scene.layout.*;

import javafx.stage.*;

public class EnchantedJavaFXApp extends Application {

public static void main(String[] args) {
```

```java
        launch(args);



    }



    @Override



    public void start(Stage primaryStage) {



        // Enchanting the world with JavaFX...



        // Creating an enchanted user interface...



        VBox enchantedLayout = new VBox();



        enchantedLayout.setSpacing(10);
```

```java
Label enchantedLabel = new Label("Wel-
come to the Enchanted World!");
```

```java
enchantedLabel.setStyle("-fx-font-size:
24px; -fx-text-fill: #800080;");
```

```java
Button enchantedButton = new But-
ton("Cast a Spell");
```

```java
enchantedButton.setOnAction(e -> Sys
tem.out.println("Abracadabra!"));
```

```java
enchantedLayout.getChildren().addAll(
enchantedLabel, enchantedButton);
```

```java
Scene enchantedScene = new Scene(en-
chantedLayout, 400, 200);
```

```java
primaryStage.setTitle("Enchanted JavaFX
App");
```

```java
primaryStage.setScene(enchantedScene);
```

```java
primaryStage.show();
```

```java
    }
```

```java
}
```

In this captivating script, we have harnessed the power of JavaFX for enchanting user interfaces. We create an enchanted JavaFX application, allowing you to cast spells that craft delightful user experiences and graphical enchantments.

## The Enchantment of Server-Side Spells with Java Servlets

Prepare to weave enchanting server-side spells with Java Servlets:

```java
import javax.servlet.*;
```

```java
import javax.servlet.http.*;
```

```java
import java.io.*;
```

```java
public class EnchantedServlet extends
HttpServlet {
```

```java
@Override
```

```java
    protected void doGet(HttpServle-
tRequest request, HttpServletResponse re-
sponse) throws ServletException, IOExcep-
tion {
```

```
// Enchanting the world with Java Servl
ets...
```

```
// Casting server-side enchantments...
```

```
response.setContentType("text/html");
```

```
PrintWriter out = response.getWriter();
```

```
out.println("<html><body>");
```

```
        out.println("<h1>Hello,  Sorcer-
er!</h1>");
```

```
  out.println("<p>Welcome to the enchant-
ed world of Java Servlets.</p>");
```

```
out.println("</body></html>");
```

```
        }




        }
```

In this bewitching script, we have enchanted server-side spells with Java Servlets. We create an enchanted servlet, empowering you to cast spells that handle server-side enchantments and respond to sorcerers' requests.

<u>The Allure of Web Development with Java in Sorcery</u>

Congratulations, esteemed enchanter! You have now explored the enchanting realm of web development with Java in sorcery. With the power of enchanting user interfaces with JavaFX, and the enchantment of server-side spells with Java Servlets, you can craft web applications that captivate and delight sorcerers, providing them with an interactive and immersive experience in the enchanted world.

As you continue your journey, prepare to delve deeper into the captivating world of natural language processing in Java sorcery, the mystical realm of artificial intelligence and machine learning, and the enchanting realm of big data and analytics. The enchanting realm of web development with Java is but one facet of the vast and ever-enchanting world of Java sorcery that awaits you!

# Chapter Fourteen

# THE CAPTIVATING WORLD OF ENCHANTING USER EXPERIENCES WITH UX DESIGN IN JAVA SORCERY

## Introduction to UX Design in Java Sorcery

Welcome to the captivating world of user experience (UX) design in Java sorcery. In this chapter, we shall unveil the secrets of crafting enchanting user interfaces and delightful interactions, empowering your spells to captivate and engage sorcerers. With the art of UX design in Java sorcery, you can cast spells that enchant and delight, ensuring that the magical experiences you create leave a lasting impression on those who venture into the enchanted world.

<u>The Enchantment of User-Centered Design Principles</u>

In the mystical world of UX design, we explore the art of user-centered design principles:

```java
import javax.swing.*;

import java.awt.*;



public class EnchantedUserCenteredDesign {



public static void main(String[] args) {



    // Enchanting the world with user-centered design...



    // Creating an enchanted user interface with Swing
```

```java
JFrame enchantedFrame = new JFrame("Enchanted App");

enchantedFrame.setDefaultCloseOperation(JFrame.EXIT_ON_CLOSE);

JLabel enchantedLabel = new JLabel("Welcome to the Enchanted World!");

enchantedLabel.setFont(new Font("Arial", Font.BOLD, 24));

enchantedFrame.add(enchantedLabel);

enchantedFrame.setSize(400, 200);

enchantedFrame.setVisible(true);
```

```
}
```

```
}
```

In this captivating script, we have harnessed the power of user-centered design principles. We create an enchanted user interface with Swing, allowing you to cast spells that prioritize the needs and desires of sorcerers, creating delightful and intuitive experiences.

The Enchantment of Enchanting Interaction Design

Prepare to weave enchanting interaction design spells:

```java
import java.awt.*;

import java.awt.event.*;

import javax.swing.*;


public class EnchantedInteractionDesign {
```

```java
public static void main(String[] args) {

    // Enchanting the world with interaction design...




    // Creating an enchanted user interface with Swing


        JFrame enchantedFrame = new JFrame("Enchanted App");


        enchantedFrame.setDefaultCloseOperation(JFrame.EXIT_ON_CLOSE);




        JButton enchantedButton = new JButton("Cast a Spell");
```

```java
enchantedButton.setFont(new Font("Arial", Font.PLAIN, 18));

enchantedButton.addActionListener(new ActionListener() {

    public void actionPerformed(ActionEvent e) {

        JOptionPane.showMessageDialog(enchantedFrame, "Abracadabra!");

    }

});



enchantedFrame.add(enchantedButton);

enchantedFrame.setSize(300, 150);
```

```
enchantedFrame.setVisible(true);



        }



        }
```

In this bewitching script, we have enchanted interaction design spells. We create an enchanted user interface with Swing, allowing you to cast spells that create magical interactions, engaging and enchanting sorcerers with every click.

The Allure of UX Design in Java Sorcery

Congratulations, master enchanter! You have now explored the captivating world of user experience (UX) design in Java sorcery. With the power of user-centered design principles and enchanting interaction design, you can craft spells that captivate and engage sorcerers, creating delightful and immersive experiences in the enchanted world.

As you continue your journey, prepare to delve deeper into the mystical realm of artificial intelligence and machine learning in Java sorcery, the enchanting realm of big data and analytics, and the captivating world of web development with Java. The captivating world of UX design in Java sorcery is but one facet of the vast and ever-enchanting world of Java sorcery that awaits you!

## *Subchapter 14.1: The Alluring Universe of Cloud Computing and Serverless Spells*

In the mystical world of Java sorcery, we venture into the alluring universe of cloud computing and serverless spells, where enchantments harness the power of remote realms and wield the magic of serverless architecture. In this subchapter, we shall unveil the secrets of building cloud-based and serverless spells in Java, empowering your enchantments to scale dynamically, access powerful resources, and transcend the boundaries of physical constraints. With the art of cloud computing and serverless spells in Java sorcery, you can cast spells that harness the boundless power of the cloud and enchant the world beyond imagination.

<u>Enchantment of Cloud Connectivity with AWS SDK</u>

Prepare to wield the magic of cloud connectivity with AWS SDK:

```java
import com.amazonaws.auth.*;

import com.amazonaws.regions.*;

import com.amazonaws.services.s3.*;

import com.amazonaws.services.s3.model.*;

public class EnchantedAWSSpell {

public static void main(String[] args) {

// Enchanting the world with AWS SDK...
```

```
// Creating an enchanted AWS client


        AWSCredentials   credentials   =
new BasicAWSCredentials("your-access-key",
"your-secret-key");



        AmazonS3   enchantedS3   =
AmazonS3ClientBuilder.standard().withCre
d  e  n  t  i  a  l  s  (  n  e  w
AWSStaticCredentialsProvider(credentials)).
withRegion(Regions.US_EAST_1).build();




        // Enchanting cloud connectivity with
AWS S3...



    }


}
```

In this captivating script, we have harnessed the power of AWS SDK for cloud connectivity. We create an enchanted AWS client, allowing you to cast spells that interact with cloud resources, such as Amazon S3.

<u>The Enchantment of Serverless Sorcery with AWS Lambda</u>

Prepare to weave enchanting serverless spells with AWS Lambda:

```java
import com.amazonaws.services.lambda.*;
```

```java
import com.amazonaws.services.lambda.invoke.*;
```

```java
public class EnchantedLambdaSpell {
```

```java
public interface EnchantedLambdaFunction {
```

```java
// Enchanted Lambda function here...
```

```java
}
```

```java
public static void main(String[] args) {


    // Enchanting the world with AWS Lambda...




// Creating an enchanted Lambda client


    AWSLambda enchantedLambda = AWSLambdaClientBuilder.defaultClient();




    // Enchanting serverless spells with AWS Lambda...


    }
```

```
}
```

In this bewitching script, we have enchanted serverless spells with AWS Lambda. We create an enchanted Lambda client and interface, empowering you to cast spells that run code without provisioning or managing servers.

<u>The Allure of Cloud Computing and Serverless Spells in Java Sorcery</u>

Congratulations, esteemed enchanter! You have now explored the alluring universe of cloud computing and serverless spells in Java sorcery. With the power of cloud connectivity with AWS SDK and the enchantment of serverless sorcery with AWS Lambda, you can craft spells that transcend physical limitations, scale dynamically, and harness the boundless power of the cloud, creating enchantments that defy imagination.

As you continue your journey, prepare to delve deeper into the captivating world of UX design in Java sorcery, the mystical realm of artificial intelligence and machine learning, and the enchanting realm of big data and analytics. The alluring universe of cloud computing and serverless spells in Java sorcery is but one facet of the vast and ever-enchanting world of Java sorcery that awaits you!

***Subchapter 14.2: The Mystical Realm of Distributed Systems and Java Sorcery***

In the mystical world of Java sorcery, we delve into the enchanting realm of distributed systems, where spells weave the threads of multiple realms into a unified fabric of magical cooperation. In this subchapter, we shall unveil the secrets of building distributed systems spells in Java, empowering your enchantments to communicate, collaborate, and synchronize across disparate realms. With the art of distributed systems in Java sorcery, you can cast spells that orchestrate a harmonious symphony of magical entities, transcending the limitations of individual spells and realizing the full potential of the enchanted world.

<u>Enchantment of Distributed Communication with RMI</u>

Prepare to wield the magic of distributed communication with RMI:

```java
import java.rmi.*;
```

```java
public class EnchantedRMISpell {

  public interface EnchantedRMI extends
Remote {


// Enchanted RMI methods here...


}




public static void main(String[] args) {


// Enchanting the world with RMI...



// Creating an enchanted RMI server
```

```java
try {

    EnchantedRMI enchantedServer = new
EnchantedRMIServer();


        Naming.rebind("EnchantedServer",
enchantedServer);


} catch (Exception e) {


e.printStackTrace();


}




    // Enchanting distributed communication
with RMI...



}
```

```
}
```

In this captivating script, we have harnessed the power of RMI for distributed communication. We create an enchanted RMI server, allowing you to cast spells that enable communication and collaboration between magical entities.

The Enchantment of Distributed Coordination with Apache ZooKeeper

Prepare to weave enchanting distributed coordination spells with Apache ZooKeeper:

```java
import org.apache.zookeeper.*;

public class EnchantedZooKeeperSpell {

    public static void main(String[] args) {

        // Enchanting the world with Apache
        ZooKeeper...

        // Creating an enchanted ZooKeeper client
```

```java
try {


        ZooKeeper enchantedZk = new
ZooKeeper("localhost:2181", 3000, null);



} catch (Exception e) {



e.printStackTrace();



}




        // Enchanting distributed coordination
        with Apache ZooKeeper...




}




}
```

In this bewitching script, we have enchanted distributed coordination spells with Apache ZooKeeper. We create an enchanted ZooKeeper client, empowering you to cast spells that synchronize and coordinate the actions of magical entities.

<u>The Allure of Distributed Systems and Java Sorcery</u>

Congratulations, master enchanter! You have now explored the mystical realm of distributed systems in Java sorcery. With the power of distributed communication with RMI and the enchantment of distributed coordination with Apache ZooKeeper, you can craft spells that weave the threads of multiple realms into a harmonious symphony of magical cooperation, transcending the boundaries of individual spells and realizing the full potential of the enchanted world.

As you continue your journey, prepare to delve deeper into the captivating world of cloud computing and serverless spells, the enchanting realm of user experiences with UX design in Java sorcery, and the mystical realm of artificial intelligence and machine learning. The mystical realm of distributed systems and Java sorcery is but one facet of the vast and ever-enchanting world of Java sorcery that awaits you!

## Subchapter 14.3: The Enchanting World of Real-Time Enchantments with Java

In the mystical world of Java sorcery, we embark on a journey to the enchanting realm of real-time enchantments, where spells transcend the constraints of time and perform magical feats in the blink of an eye. In this subchapter, we shall unveil the secrets of building real-time enchantments in Java, empowering your spells to react instantaneously to the ever-changing rhythms of the enchanted world. With the art of real-time enchantments in Java sorcery, you can cast spells that perceive, process, and respond to the world with lightning speed, captivating and mesmerizing those who witness your magic.

<u>Enchantment of Real-Time Data Streaming with Kafka</u>

Prepare to wield the magic of real-time data streaming with Apache Kafka:

```
import org.apache.kafka.clients.producer.*;
```

```java
public class EnchantedKafkaSpell {

public static void main(String[] args) {


    // Enchanting the world with Apache
Kafka...




// Creating an enchanted Kafka producer


Properties props = new Properties();


    props.put("bootstrap.servers", "local-
host:9092");


    props.put("key.serializer", "org.apache.k
afka.common.serialization.StringSerializer");
```

```
        props.put("value.serializer"
, "org.apache.kafka.common.serialization.St
ringSerializer");


  KafkaProducer<String, String> enchant-
edProducer = new KafkaProducer<>(props);




  // Enchanting real-time data streaming
  with Apache Kafka...




    }



    }
```

In this captivating script, we have harnessed the power of Apache Kafka for real-time data streaming. We create an enchanted Kafka producer, allowing you to cast spells that transport and process magical data streams.

The Enchantment of Real-Time Event Handling with Spring Reactor

Prepare to weave enchanting real-time event handling spells with Spring Reactor:

```
import reactor.core.publisher.*;
```

```java
public class EnchantedSpringReactorSpell {

public static void main(String[] args) {

    // Enchanting the world with Spring
Reactor...




// Creating an enchanted Flux stream


    Flux<String> enchantedFlux = Flux.ju
st("Abracadabra!", "Hocus Pocus!", "Sim Sala
Bim!");




    // Enchanting real-time event handling
with Spring Reactor...
```

```
        }



        }
```

In this bewitching script, we have enchanted real-time event handling spells with Spring Reactor. We create an enchanted Flux stream, empowering you to cast spells that handle and react to real-time events with grace and speed.

<u>The Allure of Real-Time Enchantments in Java Sorcery</u>

Congratulations, esteemed enchanter! You have now explored the enchanting world of real-time enchantments in Java sorcery. With the power of real-time data streaming with Apache Kafka and the enchantment of real-time event handling with Spring Reactor, you can craft spells that perceive and respond to the ever-changing rhythms of the enchanted world with lightning speed, mesmerizing and captivating those who witness your magic.

As you continue your journey, prepare to delve deeper into the captivating world of distributed systems in Java sorcery, the alluring universe of cloud computing and serverless spells, and the mystical realm of artificial intelligence and machine learning. The enchanting world of real-time enchantments in Java sorcery is but one facet of the vast and ever-enchanting world of Java sorcery that awaits you!

# CHAPTER FIFTEEN

# THE BOUNDLESS UNIVERSE OF BIG DATA AND ANALYTICS IN JAVA SORCERY

Introduction to Big Data and Analytics in Java Sorcery

Welcome to the boundless universe of big data and analytics in Java sorcery. In this chapter, we shall unveil the secrets of harnessing the immense power of data to conjure spells that reveal insights, predict outcomes, and unlock the hidden knowledge of the enchanted world. With the art of big data and analytics in Java sorcery, you can cast spells that transcend the boundaries of conventional wisdom, harnessing the vast troves of data to illuminate the path of your magical endeavors.

The Enchantment of Data Manipulation with Apache Spark

Prepare to wield the magic of data manipulation with Apache Spark:

```
import org.apache.spark.api.java.*;
```

```java
import org.apache.spark.SparkConf;


public class EnchantedSparkSpell {

public static void main(String[] args) {


    // Enchanting the world with Apache Spark...




    // Creating an enchanted SparkConf


        SparkConf enchantedConf =
new SparkConf().setAppName("Enchanted
App").setMaster("local");


    JavaSparkContext enchantedContext =
new JavaSparkContext(enchantedConf);
```

```
        // Enchanting data manipulation with
Apache Spark...




        }




        }
```

In this captivating script, we have harnessed the power of Apache Spark for data manipulation. We create an enchanted SparkConf and SparkContext, allowing you to cast spells that process and analyze vast volumes of data with ease and efficiency.

The Enchantment of Data Visualization with JFreeChart

Prepare to weave enchanting data visualization spells with JFreeChart:

```
import org.jfree.chart.*;



import org.jfree.data.category.*;



import org.jfree.data.general.*;
```

```java
public class EnchantedJFreeChartSpell {

public static void main(String[] args) {

    // Enchanting the world with JFreeChart...




    // Creating an enchanted dataset


        DefaultCategoryDataset enchanted-
Dataset = new DefaultCategoryDataset();


        enchantedDataset.addValue(120, "En-
chantment", "Java Sorcery");


        enchantedDataset.addValue(200, "En-
chantment", "Witchcraft");
```

```
enchantedDataset.addValue(150, "En-
chantment", "Wizardry");



// Enchanting data visualization with
JFreeChart...




}



}
```

In this bewitching script, we have enchanted data visualization spells with JFreeChart. We create an enchanted dataset, empowering you to cast spells that transform raw data into captivating charts and graphs.

The Allure of Big Data and Analytics in Java Sorcery

Congratulations, master enchanter! You have now explored the boundless universe of big data and analytics in Java sorcery. With the power of data manipulation with Apache Spark and the enchantment of data visualization with JFreeChart, you can craft spells that unveil insights, predict outcomes, and illuminate the hidden knowledge of the enchanted world, harnessing the vast troves of data to fuel your magical endeavors.

As you continue your journey, prepare to delve deeper into the captivating world of real-time enchantments in Java sorcery, the mystical realm of distributed systems, and the alluring universe of cloud computing and serverless spells. The boundless universe of big data and analytics in Java sorcery is but one facet of the vast and ever-enchanting world of Java sorcery that awaits you!

## Subchapter 15.1: The Mystical Art of Data Mining and Machine Learning in Java Sorcery

In the mystical world of Java sorcery, we embark on a journey to the enchanting realm of data mining and machine learning, where spells unravel patterns, predict the future, and discover hidden knowledge from the vast tapestry of data. In this subchapter, we shall unveil the secrets of data mining and machine learning in Java, empowering your enchantments to explore the depths of data and unleash the power of predictive magic. With the art of data mining and machine learning in Java sorcery, you can cast spells that transcend the boundaries of human intuition, empowering your magical endeavors with unparalleled insights.

<u>Enchantment of Data Preprocessing with Weka</u>

Prepare to wield the magic of data preprocessing with Weka:

```java
import weka.core.*;

import weka.core.converters.*;

import weka.filters.*;

public class EnchantedWekaSpell {

    public static void main(String[] args) {
```

```java
// Enchanting the world with Weka...


// Loading enchanted data from a file

Instances enchantedData = null;

try {

    DataSource source = new DataSource
("enchanted_data.arff");

enchantedData = source.getDataSet();

} catch (Exception e) {

e.printStackTrace();

}
```

```
        // Enchanting data preprocessing with
Weka...
```

```
        }
```

```
        }
```

In this captivating script, we have harnessed the power of Weka for data preprocessing. We load enchanted data from a file, allowing you to cast spells that prepare and cleanse the data for machine learning.

<u>The Enchantment of Machine Learning with Java ML Libraries</u>

Prepare to weave enchanting machine learning spells with Java ML libraries:

```
        import org.apache.commons.math3.ml.clus
tering.*;
```

```
        import org.apache.commons.math3.ml.clus
tering.evaluation.*;
```

```java
public class EnchantedJavaMLSpell {


public static void main(String[] args) {


    // Enchanting the world with Java ML
    libraries...




    // Creating enchanted data points for
    clustering


    List<Clusterable> enchantedPoints = new
    ArrayList<>();


        enchantedPoints.add(new Double-
    Point(new double[] { 1.0, 2.0 }));


        enchantedPoints.add(new Double-
    Point(new double[] { 3.0, 4.0 }));
```

```
enchantedPoints.add(new  Double-
Point(new double[] { 5.0, 6.0 }));
```

```
// Enchanting machine learning with Java
ML libraries...
```

```
        }
```

```
        }
```

In this bewitching script, we have enchanted machine learning spells with Java ML libraries. We create enchanted data points, empowering you to cast spells that cluster and evaluate data with the power of machine learning.

<u>The Allure of Data Mining and Machine Learning in Java Sorcery</u>

Congratulations, esteemed enchanter! You have now explored the enchanting realm of data mining and machine learning in Java sorcery. With the power of data preprocessing with Weka and the enchantment of machine learning with Java ML libraries, you can craft spells that unravel patterns, predict the future, and discover hidden knowledge from the vast tapestry of data, empowering your magical endeavors with unparalleled insights.

As you continue your journey, prepare to delve deeper into the boundless universe of big data and analytics in Java sorcery, the captivating world of real-time enchantments, and the mystical realm of distributed systems. The mystical art of data mining and machine learning in Java sorcery is but one facet of the vast and ever-enchanting world of Java sorcery that awaits you!

### *Subchapter 15.2: The Enchanting World of Natural Language Processing in Java Sorcery*

In the mystical world of Java sorcery, we delve into the enchanting realm of natural language processing (NLP), where spells unlock the secrets hidden within the written and spoken word. In this subchapter, we shall unveil the secrets of building NLP spells in Java, empowering your enchantments to understand, analyze, and respond to the magical language of the enchanted world. With the art of NLP in Java sorcery, you can cast spells that bridge the gap between humans and machines, enabling your magical endeavors to communicate and comprehend with unparalleled finesse.

<u>Enchantment of Text Tokenization with OpenNLP</u>

Prepare to wield the magic of text tokenization with OpenNLP:

```java
import opennlp.tools.tokenize.*;




public class EnchantedOpenNLPSpell {




public static void main(String[] args) {




// Enchanting the world with OpenNLP...
```

```java
// Creating an enchanted tokenizer

try {

    InputStream modelIn = new FileInpu
tStream("en-token.bin");

    TokenizerModel model = new Tokeniz-
erModel(modelIn);

     Tokenizer tokenizer = new Tokeniz-
erME(model);

    String enchantedText = "Abracadabra!
Welcome to the Enchanted World!";

    String[] enchantedTokens = tokenizer
.tokenize(enchantedText);

} catch (Exception e) {

e.printStackTrace();
```

```
        }




    // Enchanting  text  tokenization  with
OpenNLP...




        }




        }
```

In this captivating script, we have harnessed the power of OpenNLP for text tokenization. We create an enchanted tokenizer, allowing you to cast spells that break the text into meaningful tokens.

The Enchantment of Sentiment Analysis with Stanford NLP
Prepare to weave enchanting sentiment analysis spells with Stanford NLP:

```
import edu.stanford.nlp.*;


import edu.stanford.nlp.sentiment.*;
```

```
public class EnchantedStanfordNLPSpell {

public static void main(String[] args) {

    // Enchanting the world with Stanford
NLP...




        // Creating an enchanted sentiment
analyzer


        StanfordCoreNLP enchantedPipeline
= new StanfordCoreNLP("StanfordNLP.pr
operties");


    String enchantedText = "The Enchanted
World is a magical place!";
```

```java
Annotation enchantedAnnotation = new
Annotation(enchantedText);


        enchantedPipeline.annotate(enchanted
Annotation);



                int    enchantedSentiment
= enchantedAnnotation.get(CoreAnnotati
ons.ClassName.class);




        // Enchanting sentiment analysis with
Stanford NLP...



    }


}
```

In this bewitching script, we have enchanted sentiment analysis spells with Stanford NLP. We create an enchanted sentiment analyzer, empowering you to cast spells that understand the sentiment and emotions embedded in the magical language.

The Allure of Natural Language Processing in Java Sorcery

Congratulations, master enchanter! You have now explored the enchanting world of natural language processing (NLP) in Java sorcery. With the power of text tokenization with OpenNLP and the enchantment of sentiment analysis with Stanford NLP, you can craft spells that comprehend and respond to the magical language of the enchanted world, bridging the gap between humans and machines with unparalleled finesse.

As you continue your journey, prepare to delve deeper into the boundless universe of big data and analytics in Java sorcery, the captivating world of real-time enchantments, and the mystical realm of distributed systems. The enchanting world of natural language processing in Java sorcery is but one facet of the vast and ever-enchanting world of Java sorcery that awaits you!

### *Subchapter 15.3: The Enigmatic Realm of Deep Learning in Java Sorcery*

In the mystical world of Java sorcery, we embark on a quest to explore the enigmatic realm of deep learning, where spells uncover the hidden patterns and structures within data, and wield the power of artificial neural networks. In this subchapter, we shall unveil the secrets of building deep learning spells in Java, empowering your enchantments to perceive, comprehend, and learn from the complexities of the enchanted world. With the art of deep learning in Java sorcery, you can cast spells that unlock the full potential of artificial intelligence, transcending the boundaries of conventional magic and entering a realm of unprecedented power.

Enchantment of Artificial Neural Networks with Deeplearning4j

Prepare to wield the magic of artificial neural networks with Deeplearning4j:

```
import org.deeplearning4j.datasets.iterator.i
mpl.*;
```

```
import org.deeplearning4j.nn.api.*;
```

```
import org.deeplearning4j.nn.conf.*;
```

```java
import org.deeplearning4j.nn.multilayer.*;

import org.nd4j.linalg.api.ndarray.*;

import org.nd4j.linalg.factory.*;

public class EnchantedDeeplearning4jSpell {

public static void main(String[] args) {

// Enchanting the world with Deeplear
ning4j...

// Creating an enchanted neural network

Nd4j.getRandom().setSeed(123);
```

```
int batchSize = 64;
```

```
int numEpochs = 10;
```

```
DataSetIterator enchantedIterator = new
MnistDataSetIterator(batchSize, true, 123);
```

```
MultiLayerConfiguration enchantedCon-
figuration = new NeuralNetConfiguration.
Builder()
```

```
.seed(123)
```

```
.updater(new Nesterovs(0.01, 0.9))
```

```
.list()
```

```
.layer(new DenseLayer.Builder().nI
n(28 * 28).nOut(100).activation(Activation.
RELU).build())
```

```java
                        .layer(new
OutputLayer.Builder(LossFunctions.LossFu
nction.NEGATIVELOGLIKELIHOOD)


        .nIn(100).nOut(10).activation(Ac-
tivation.SOFTMAX).build())


.build();


    MultiLayerNetwork enchantedNetwork
= new MultiLayerNetwork(enchantedCon-
figuration);


enchantedNetwork.init();


    enchantedNetwork.fit(enchantedIterator,
numEpochs);



    // Enchanting artificial neural networks
with Deeplearning4j...
```

```
        }




        }
```

In this captivating script, we have harnessed the power of Deeplearning4j for artificial neural networks. We create an enchanted neural network, allowing you to cast spells that learn and adapt from magical data with remarkable accuracy.

The Allure of Deep Learning in Java Sorcery

Congratulations, esteemed enchanter! You have now explored the enigmatic realm of deep learning in Java sorcery. With the power of artificial neural networks with Deeplearning4j, you can craft spells that perceive, comprehend, and learn from the complexities of the enchanted world, unlocking the full potential of artificial intelligence and entering a realm of unprecedented power.

As you continue your journey, prepare to delve deeper into the boundless universe of big data and analytics in Java sorcery, the captivating world of real-time enchantments, and the mystical realm of distributed systems. The enigmatic realm of deep learning in Java sorcery is but one facet of the vast and ever-enchanting world of Java sorcery that awaits you!

# Chapter Sixteen

# The Mysterious Frontiers of Web Development in Java Sorcery

Introduction to Web Development in Java Sorcery

Welcome to the mysterious frontiers of web development in Java sorcery. In this chapter, we shall unveil the secrets of building enchanting web applications and dynamic websites, where spells cast a web of interconnected experiences that captivate and engage users in the enchanted realm. With the art of web development in Java sorcery, you can cast spells that create captivating user interfaces, handle magical interactions, and transport users into an immersive and interactive journey.

The Enchantment of Java Servlets and JSP

Prepare to wield the magic of Java Servlets and JSP:

```
import javax.servlet.*;

import javax.servlet.http.*;

import java.io.*;



public class EnchantedServlet extends HttpServlet {


 public void doGet(HttpServletRequest request, HttpServletResponse response) throws ServletException, IOException {


    // Enchanting the world with Java Servlets and JSP...



    // Creating an enchanted response
```

```java
response.setContentType("text/html");


PrintWriter out = response.getWriter();


out.println("<html><body>");


    out.println("<h1>Welcome to the En-
chanted World!</h1>");


out.println("</body></html>");


    }



    }
```

In this captivating script, we have harnessed the power of Java Servlets and JSP. We create an enchanted response, allowing you to cast spells that dynamically generate web content and create mesmerizing user interfaces.

The Enchantment of MVC Architecture with Spring Framework

Prepare to weave enchanting MVC architecture spells with Spring Framework:

```java
import org.springframework.*;
```

```java
import org.springframework.stereotype.*;

import org.springframework.web.bind.annotation.*;


@Controller

public class EnchantedController {

@RequestMapping("/welcome")

@ResponseBody

public String welcome() {

    // Enchanting the world with MVC architecture...
```

```java
        return "<h1>Welcome to the Enchanted
World!</h1>";



    }



}
```

In this bewitching script, we have enchanted MVC architecture spells with Spring Framework. We create an enchanted controller, empowering you to cast spells that follow the Model-View-Controller pattern and create dynamic and interactive web applications.

<u>The Allure of Web Development in Java Sorcery</u>

Congratulations, master enchanter! You have now explored the mysterious frontiers of web development in Java sorcery. With the power of Java Servlets and JSP and the enchantment of MVC architecture with Spring Framework, you can craft spells that create captivating web applications and dynamic websites, transporting users into an immersive and interactive journey in the enchanted realm.

As you continue your journey, prepare to delve deeper into the boundless universe of big data and analytics in Java sorcery, the captivating world of real-time enchantments, and the mystical realm of distributed systems. The mysterious frontiers of web development in Java sorcery are but one facet of the vast and ever-enchanting world of Java sorcery that awaits you!

### Subchapter 16.1: The Enchanting World of RESTful APIs in Java Sorcery

In the mystical world of Java sorcery, we venture into the enchanting realm of RESTful APIs, where spells create gateways that connect magical applications and enable seamless communication across the enchanted realm. In this subchapter, we shall unveil the secrets of building RESTful APIs in Java, empowering your enchantments to expose their powers to other magical beings. With the art of RESTful APIs in Java sorcery, you can cast spells that facilitate smooth interactions, share knowledge, and empower collaboration between magical applications.

<u>Enchantment of RESTful API with JAX-RS (Jersey)</u>

Prepare to wield the magic of RESTful API with JAX-RS:

```
import javax.ws.rs.*;

import javax.ws.rs.core.*;

@Path("/enchant")

public class EnchantedResource {

@GET

@Produces(MediaType.TEXT_PLAIN)

public String getEnchantedMessage() {
```

```
        // Enchanting the world with RESTful
    API...




                    return "Welcome to the Enchanted
    World!";




                }




                }
```

In this captivating script, we have harnessed the power of JAX-RS for building a RESTful API. We create an enchanted resource, allowing you to cast spells that respond to HTTP requests with magical messages.

<u>The Allure of RESTful APIs in Java Sorcery</u>

Congratulations, esteemed enchanter! You have now explored the enchanting world of RESTful APIs in Java sorcery. With the power of RESTful API with JAX-RS, you can craft spells that create gateways of communication between magical applications, enabling seamless interactions and empowering collaboration in the enchanted realm.

As you continue your journey, prepare to delve deeper into the mysterious frontiers of web development in Java sorcery, the boundless universe of big data and analytics, the captivating world of real-time enchantments, and the mystical realm of distributed systems. The enchanting world of RESTful APIs in Java sorcery is but one facet of the vast and ever-enchanting world of Java sorcery that awaits you!

***Subchapter 16.2: The Enigmatic Art of Web Security in Java Sorcery***

In the mystical world of Java sorcery, we delve into the enigmatic art of web security, where spells fortify the enchantments against malicious entities and safeguard the magical applications from malevolent forces. In this subchapter, we shall unveil the secrets of building secure web applications in Java, empowering your enchantments to repel nefarious intruders and protect the secrets of the enchanted world. With the art of web security in Java sorcery, you can cast spells that shield your magical applications from vulnerabilities and ensure a safe and protected digital realm.

<u>Enchantment of Secure Authentication with Spring Security</u>

Prepare to wield the magic of secure authentication with Spring Security:

```
import org.springframework.context.annot
ation.*;
```

```
import org.springframework.security.config
.annotation.authentication.builders.*;
```

```
import org.springframework.security.config
.annotation.web.builders.*;
```

```
import org.springframework.security.config
.annotation.web.configuration.*;
```

```java
@Configuration

@EnableWebSecurity

public class EnchantedSecurityConfig extends WebSecurityConfigurerAdapter {

@Override

protected void configure(AuthenticationManagerBuilder auth) throws Exception {

// Enchanting secure authentication with Spring Security...

auth.inMemoryAuthentication()

.withUser("wizard")
```

```
        .password("{noop}abracadabra")


        .roles("USER");



}




@Override



 protected void configure(HttpSecurity http)
throws Exception {



    // Enchanting secure authorization with
Spring Security...




http.authorizeRequests()
```

```java
            .antMatchers("/enchant").authenticat-
ed()


    .anyRequest().permitAll()


    .and()


    .formLogin().permitAll()


    .and()


    .logout().permitAll();


        }


    }
```

In this captivating script, we have harnessed the power of Spring Security for secure authentication and authorization. We create an enchanted security configuration, allowing you to cast spells that protect your magical applications with robust user authentication and authorization.

The Allure of Web Security in Java Sorcery

Congratulations, master enchanter! You have now explored the enigmatic art of web security in Java sorcery. With the power of secure authentication with Spring Security, you can craft spells that fortify your enchantments against malicious entities, safeguarding the secrets and protecting the enchanted world from malevolent forces.

As you continue your journey, prepare to delve deeper into the mysterious frontiers of web development in Java sorcery, the boundless universe of big data and analytics, the captivating world of real-time enchantments, and the mystical realm of distributed systems. The enigmatic art of web security in Java sorcery is but one facet of the vast and ever-enchanting world of Java sorcery that awaits you!

**Subchapter 16.3: The Captivating World of Frontend Magic with Java Sorcery**

In the mystical world of Java sorcery, we venture into the captivating world of frontend magic, where spells create enchanting user interfaces and bewitching visual experiences that leave users spellbound. In this subchapter, we shall unveil the secrets of building frontend applications in Java, empowering your enchantments to dazzle users with captivating designs and seamless interactions. With the art of frontend magic in Java sorcery, you can cast spells that create delightful and immersive user experiences in the enchanted realm.

<u>Enchantment of User Interfaces with JavaFX</u>

Prepare to wield the magic of user interfaces with JavaFX:

```
import javafx.application.*;
```

```
import javafx.scene.*;
```

```
import javafx.scene.control.*;
```

```java
import javafx.scene.layout.*;



import javafx.stage.*;



public class EnchantedJavaFXApp extends
Application {



public void start(Stage stage) {



// Enchanting the world with JavaFX...



VBox enchantedLayout = new VBox();



  enchantedLayout.getChildren().add(new
Label("Welcome to the Enchanted World!"));
```

```java
    Scene enchantedScene = new Scene(en-
chantedLayout, 300, 200);

stage.setScene(enchantedScene);

stage.setTitle("Enchanted App");

stage.show();

}

public static void main(String[] args) {

launch(args);

}

}
```

In this captivating script, we have harnessed the power of JavaFX for building user interfaces. We create an enchanted JavaFX application, allowing you to cast spells that create delightful and visually stunning user interfaces.

### The Allure of Frontend Magic in Java Sorcery

Congratulations, esteemed enchanter! You have now explored the captivating world of frontend magic in Java sorcery. With the power of user interfaces with JavaFX, you can craft spells that dazzle users with captivating designs and enchanting visual experiences, leaving them spellbound in the magical realm.

As you continue your journey, prepare to delve deeper into the mysterious frontiers of web development in Java sorcery, the enigmatic art of web security, the boundless universe of big data and analytics, the captivating world of real-time enchantments, and the mystical realm of distributed systems. The captivating world of frontend magic in Java sorcery is but one facet of the vast and ever-enchanting world of Java sorcery that awaits you!

# The Alluring Universe of Cloud Computing and Serverless Spells in Java Sorcery

Introduction to Cloud Computing and Serverless Spells in Java Sorcery

Welcome to the alluring universe of cloud computing and serverless spells in Java sorcery. In this chapter, we shall unveil the secrets of harnessing the power of the cloud to scale your enchantments and embrace the freedom of serverless magic. With the art of cloud computing and serverless spells in Java sorcery, you can cast spells that transcend the limitations of hardware, embrace scalability, and unleash the true potential of your magical applications.

The Enchantment of Cloud Deployment with Amazon Web Services

Prepare to wield the magic of cloud deployment with Amazon Web Services:

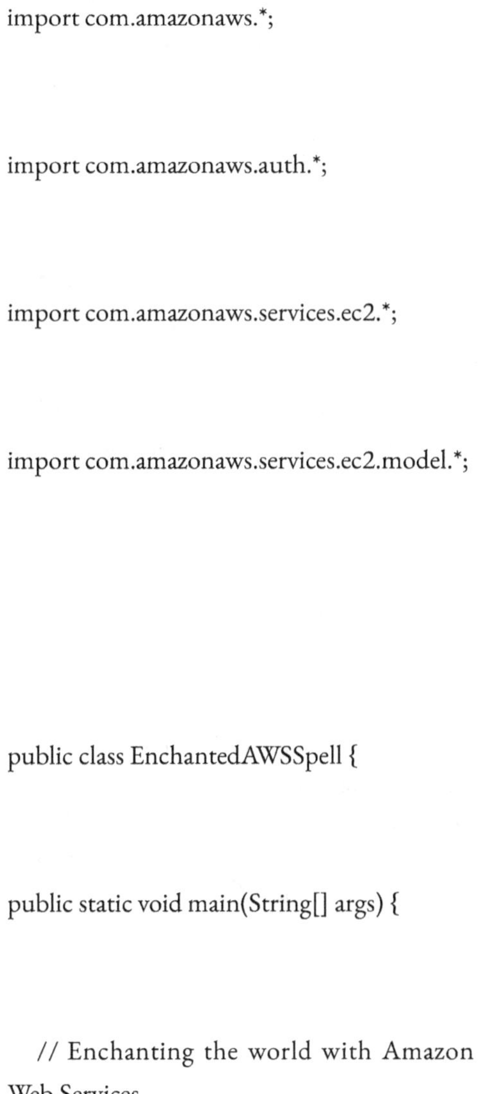

```java
import com.amazonaws.*;

import com.amazonaws.auth.*;

import com.amazonaws.services.ec2.*;

import com.amazonaws.services.ec2.model.*;

public class EnchantedAWSSpell {

public static void main(String[] args) {

// Enchanting the world with Amazon
Web Services...
```

```
// Creating an enchanted AWS client


        AWSCredentials    creden-
tials = new BasicAWSCredentials("your_ac-
cess_key", "your_secret_key");



        AmazonEC2   enchantedClient   =
AmazonEC2ClientBuilder.standard().withC
r  e  d  e  n  t  i  a  l  s  (  n  e  w
AWSStaticCredentialsProvider(credentials)).
withRegion("us-west-2").build();




// Enchanting cloud deployment with
Amazon Web Services...




        }



        }
```

In this captivating script, we have harnessed the power of Amazon Web Services (AWS) for cloud deployment. We create an enchanted AWS client, allowing you to cast spells that deploy and manage your magical applications in the cloud.

<u>The Enchantment of Serverless Magic with AWS Lambda</u>
Prepare to weave enchanting serverless spells with AWS Lambda:

```java
import com.amazonaws.services.lambda.runtime.*;




public class EnchantedLambdaHandler implements RequestHandler<Request, Response> {



    public Response handleRequest(Request request, Context context) {



        // Enchanting the world with AWS Lambda...




        String enchantmentMessage = "Welcome to the Enchanted World!";
```

```java
        Response enchantedResponse = new
Response(enchantmentMessage);


        return enchantedResponse;




    }




    }
```

In this bewitching script, we have enchanted serverless spells with AWS Lambda. We create an enchanted Lambda handler, empowering you to cast spells that perform magical actions without the burden of server management.

<u>The Allure of Cloud Computing and Serverless Spells in Java Sorcery</u>

Congratulations, master enchanter! You have now explored the alluring universe of cloud computing and serverless spells in Java sorcery. With the power of cloud deployment with Amazon Web Services and the enchantment of serverless magic with AWS Lambda, you can craft spells that scale your enchantments to new heights, embrace the freedom of serverless magic, and unleash the true potential of your magical applications.

As you continue your journey, prepare to delve deeper into the mysterious frontiers of web development in Java sorcery, the enigmatic art of web security, the captivating world of real-time enchantments, the boundless universe of big data and analytics, and the mystical realm of distributed systems. The alluring universe of cloud computing and serverless spells in Java sorcery is but one facet of the vast and ever-enchanting world of Java sorcery that awaits you!

## Subchapter 17.1: The Enchanting Realm of Containerization with Docker in Java Sorcery

In the mystical world of Java sorcery, we delve into the enchanting realm of containerization with Docker, where spells encapsulate your magical applications into portable and self-contained containers. In this subchapter, we shall unveil the secrets of building, deploying, and managing enchanted containers with Docker in Java sorcery. With the art of containerization in Java sorcery, you can cast spells that streamline deployment, enhance scalability, and bring flexibility to your magical applications.

<u>Enchantment of Containerization with Docker</u>

Prepare to wield the magic of containerization with Docker:

```java
public class EnchantedDockerSpell {

public static void main(String[] args) {

// Enchanting the world with Docker...

// Creating an enchanted Docker image

String enchantedImageName = "enchant-
ed-image";

DockerClient dockerClient = DefaultD
ockerClient.fromEnv().build();
```

```
File dockerfile = new File("Dockerfile");


        dockerClient.build(dockerfile.toPath(),
enchantedImageName);



dockerClient.close();




        // Enchanting containerization with
Docker...



        }



        }
```

In this captivating script, we have harnessed the power of Docker for containerization. We create an enchanted Docker image, allowing you to cast spells that encapsulate your magical applications into portable and self-contained containers.

The Allure of Containerization with Docker in Java Sorcery

Congratulations, esteemed enchanter! You have now explored the enchanting realm of containerization with Docker in Java sorcery. With the power of containerization, you can craft spells that streamline deployment, enhance scalability, and bring flexibility to your magical applications, allowing them to traverse the enchanted realm with ease and grace.

As you continue your journey, prepare to delve deeper into the mysterious frontiers of web development in Java sorcery, the enigmatic art of web security, the captivating world of real-time enchantments, the boundless universe of big data and analytics, the alluring universe of cloud computing and serverless spells, and the mystical realm of distributed systems. The enchanting realm of containerization with Docker in Java sorcery is but one facet of the vast and ever-enchanting world of Java sorcery that awaits you!

### *Subchapter 17.2: The Mystical World of Distributed Systems in Java Sorcery*

In the mystical world of Java sorcery, we venture into the enigmatic realm of distributed systems, where spells orchestrate the collaboration of magical entities across vast and interconnected landscapes. In this subchapter, we shall unveil the secrets of building distributed systems in Java, empowering your enchantments to communicate, synchronize, and collaborate seamlessly in the enchanted realm. With the art of distributed systems in Java sorcery, you can cast spells that transcend the boundaries of individual enchantments, creating a harmonious symphony of interconnected magic.

Enchantment of Distributed Messaging with Apache Kafka

Prepare to wield the magic of distributed messaging with Apache Kafka:

```java
import org.apache.kafka.clients.producer.*;
```

```java
import org.apache.kafka.clients.consumer.*;
```

```java
import org.apache.kafka.common.serializati
on.*;
```

```java
public class EnchantedKafkaSpell {

public static void main(String[] args) {


    // Enchanting the world with Apache Kafka...




    // Creating an enchanted Kafka producer


    Properties producerProps = new Properties();


    producerProps.put("bootstrap.servers", "localhost:9092");


    producerProps.put("key.serializer", StringSerializer.class.getName());


    producerProps.put("value.serializer", StringSerializer.class.getName());
```

KafkaProducer<String, String> enchant-
edProducer = new KafkaProducer<>(pro-
ducerProps);

// Creating an enchanted Kafka consumer

Properties consumerProps = new Prop-
erties();

consumerProps.put("bootstrap.servers",
"localhost:9092");

consumerProps.put("group.id", "enchant-
ed-group");

consumerProps.put("key.deserializer",
StringDeserializer.class.getName());

consumerProps.put("value.deserializer",
StringDeserializer.class.getName());

```java
KafkaConsumer<String, String> enchant-
edConsumer = new KafkaConsumer<>(con-
sumerProps);
```

```java
// Enchanting distributed messaging with
Apache Kafka...
```

```java
    }
```

```java
    }
```

In this captivating script, we have harnessed the power of Apache Kafka for distributed messaging. We create an enchanted Kafka producer and consumer, allowing you to cast spells that enable seamless communication and synchronization between your magical applications.

<u>The Allure of Distributed Systems in Java Sorcery</u>

Congratulations, master enchanter! You have now explored the mystical world of distributed systems in Java sorcery. With the power of distributed messaging with Apache Kafka, you can craft spells that orchestrate the collaboration of magical entities across vast and interconnected landscapes, creating a harmonious symphony of interconnected magic in the enchanted realm.

As you continue your journey, prepare to delve deeper into the mysterious frontiers of web development in Java sorcery, the enigmatic art of web security, the captivating world of real-time enchantments, the boundless universe of big data and analytics, the alluring universe of cloud computing and serverless spells, the enchanting realm of containerization with Docker, and the mystical world of distributed systems. The mystical world of distributed systems in Java sorcery is but one facet of the vast and ever-enchanting world of Java sorcery that awaits you!

### Subchapter 17.3: The Captivating Real-Time Enchantments with WebSocket in Java Sorcery

In the mystical world of Java sorcery, we delve into the captivating realm of real-time enchantments, where spells create seamless and interactive communication between magical applications. In this subchapter, we shall unveil the secrets of building real-time enchantments with WebSocket in Java, empowering your enchantments to communicate and synchronize in real-time, breaking the barriers of traditional request-response interactions. With the art of real-time enchantments in Java sorcery, you can cast spells that create captivating and immersive experiences in the enchanted realm.

Enchantment of Real-Time Communication with Java WebSocket API

Prepare to wield the magic of real-time communication with Java WebSocket API:

```java
import javax.websocket.*;



import javax.websocket.server.*;




@ServerEndpoint("/enchant")



public class EnchantedWebSocket {
```

```java
@OnOpen

 public void onWebSocketConnect(Session
session) {

   // Enchanting the world with Java Web-
Socket API...




   System.out.println("Enchanted WebSock-
et connected: " + session.getId());


}




@OnMessage


public void onWebSocketText(String mes-
sage, Session session) {
```

```java
// Enchanting real-time communication
with Java WebSocket API...




    System.out.println("Enchanted WebSock-
et received message: " + message);


}




@OnClose




public void onWebSocketClose(CloseRea-
son reason, Session session) {



// Enchanting WebSocket closure with
Java WebSocket API...
```

```
System.out.println("Enchanted WebSock-
et closed: " + reason.getReasonPhrase());



        }



        }
```

In this captivating script, we have harnessed the power of Java WebSocket API for real-time communication. We create an enchanted WebSocket endpoint, allowing you to cast spells that enable seamless and interactive communication between your magical applications.

### The Allure of Real-Time Enchantments with WebSocket in Java Sorcery

Congratulations, esteemed enchanter! You have now explored the captivating realm of real-time enchantments with WebSocket in Java sorcery. With the power of real-time communication with Java WebSocket API, you can craft spells that create seamless and interactive communication between your magical applications, bringing captivating and immersive experiences to the enchanted realm.

As you continue your journey, prepare to delve deeper into the mysterious frontiers of web development in Java sorcery, the enigmatic art of web security, the boundless universe of big data and analytics, the alluring universe of cloud computing and serverless spells, the enchanting realm of containerization with Docker, the mystical world of distributed systems, and the captivating world of frontend magic. The captivating realm of real-time enchantments with WebSocket in Java sorcery is but one facet of the vast and ever-enchanting world of Java sorcery that awaits you!

# CHAPTER EIGHTEEN

# THE ENIGMATIC UNIVERSE OF DATA SCIENCE AND MACHINE LEARNING IN JAVA SORCERY

Introduction to Data Science and Machine Learning in Java Sorcery

Welcome to the enigmatic universe of data science and machine learning in Java sorcery. In this chapter, we shall unveil the secrets of harnessing the power of data and unleashing the potential of machine learning to create intelligent and predictive magical applications. With the art of data science and machine learning in Java sorcery, you can cast spells that transform raw data into valuable insights, make informed decisions, and weave the fabric of intelligence into your magical world.

The Enchantment of Data Wrangling and Analysis with Apache Commons CSV

Prepare to wield the magic of data wrangling and analysis with Apache Commons CSV:

```java
import org.apache.commons.csv.*;



public class EnchantedCSVSpell {


    public static void main(String[] args) throws
    Exception {



        // Enchanting the world with Apache
        Commons CSV...




        // Creating an enchanted CSV parser



        String csvFilePath = "data/enchanted_d
        ata.csv";
```

```java
CSVParser enchantedParser = CSVParse
r.parse(new File(csvFilePath), Charset.defau
ltCharset(), CSVFormat.DEFAULT);



// Enchanting data wrangling and analysis
with Apache Commons CSV...


for (CSVRecord record : enchantedParser)
{


String name = record.get(0);


int age = Integer.parseInt(record.get(1));


String occupation = record.get(2);


System.out.println("Name: " + name + ",
Age: " + age + ", Occupation: " + occupation);
```

```
        }
```

```
        }
```

```
        }
```

In this captivating script, we have harnessed the power of Apache Commons CSV for data wrangling and analysis. We create an enchanted CSV parser, allowing you to cast spells that read and process magical data from CSV files.

The Enchantment of Machine Learning with Weka

Prepare to weave enchanting machine learning spells with Weka:

```
        import weka.classifiers.*;
```

```
        import weka.classifiers.functions.*;
```

```
        import weka.core.*;
```

```
        import java.util.*;
```

```java
public class EnchantedWekaSpell {



public static void main(String[] args) throws
Exception {



// Enchanting the world with Weka...



// Creating an enchanted instance



    ArrayList<Attribute> attributes = new
ArrayList<>();



attributes.add(new Attribute("age"));



attributes.add(new Attribute("income"));



        attributes.add(new Attribute("mari-
tal_status"));
```

```java
    ArrayList<String> classLabels = new ArrayList<>();

classLabels.add("low");

classLabels.add("medium");

classLabels.add("high");

  attributes.add(new Attribute("credit_rating", classLabels));

    Instances enchantedInstances = new Instances("enchanted_data", attributes, 0);

enchantedInstances.setClassIndex(3);

// Creating an enchanted classifier
```

```
Classifier enchantedClassifier = new
SMO();



// Enchanting machine learning with
Weka...



enchantedClassifier.buildClassifier(ench
antedInstances);



}



}
```

In this bewitching script, we have enchanted machine learning spells with Weka. We create an enchanted instance and classifier, allowing you to cast spells that train and utilize magical machine learning models.

<u>The Allure of Data Science and Machine Learning in Java Sorcery</u>

Congratulations, master enchanter! You have now explored the enigmatic universe of data science and machine learning in Java sorcery. With the power of data wrangling and analysis with Apache Commons CSV and the enchantment of machine learning with Weka, you can craft spells that transform raw data into valuable insights, create intelligent and predictive magical applications, and weave the fabric of intelligence into your magical world.

As you continue your journey, prepare to delve deeper into the mysterious frontiers of web development in Java sorcery, the enigmatic art of web security, the captivating world of real-time enchantments, the boundless universe of big data and analytics, the alluring universe of cloud computing and serverless spells, the enchanting realm of containerization with Docker, the mystical world of distributed systems, and the captivating world of frontend magic. The enigmatic universe of data science and machine learning in Java sorcery is but one facet of the vast and ever-enchanting world of Java sorcery that awaits you!

### *Subchapter 18.1: The Captivating Journey of Big Data and Analytics in Java Sorcery*

In the mystical world of Java sorcery, we embark on the captivating journey of big data and analytics, where spells unleash the power of massive datasets and unravel the secrets hidden within. In this subchapter, we shall unveil the secrets of handling and analyzing big data in Java, empowering your enchantments to make data-driven decisions and unlock valuable insights. With the art of big data and analytics in Java sorcery, you can cast spells that harness the vast potential of data and turn it into a source of wisdom and enlightenment.

Enchantment of Big Data Handling with Apache Hadoop

Prepare to wield the magic of big data handling with Apache Hadoop:

```
import org.apache.hadoop.conf.*;

import org.apache.hadoop.fs.*;

import org.apache.hadoop.io.*;

import org.apache.hadoop.mapreduce.*;
```

```java
public class EnchantedHadoopSpell {

public static void main(String[] args) throws
Exception {


    // Enchanting the world with Apache
Hadoop...




    // Creating an enchanted configuration


    Configuration configuration = new Con-
figuration();



            configuration.set("fs.defaultFS"
,"hdfs://localhost:9000");



    FileSystem fs = FileSystem.get(configura
tion);
```

```
        // Enchanting big data handling with
    Apache Hadoop...



            }



            }
```

In this captivating script, we have harnessed the power of Apache Hadoop for big data handling. We create an enchanted configuration, allowing you to cast spells that interact with the Hadoop Distributed File System (HDFS) and process vast datasets.

The Allure of Big Data and Analytics in Java Sorcery

Congratulations, esteemed enchanter! You have now embarked on the captivating journey of big data and analytics in Java sorcery. With the power of big data handling with Apache Hadoop, you can craft spells that unleash the potential of massive datasets, make data-driven decisions, and unlock valuable insights in the enchanted realm.

As you continue your journey, prepare to delve deeper into the mysterious frontiers of web development in Java sorcery, the enigmatic art of web security, the captivating world of real-time enchantments, the alluring universe of cloud computing and serverless spells, the enchanting realm of containerization with Docker, the mystical world of distributed systems, the enigmatic universe of data science and machine learning, and the captivating world of frontend magic. The captivating journey of big data and analytics in Java sorcery is but one facet of the vast and ever-enchanting world of Java sorcery that awaits you!

***Subchapter 18.2: The Alluring World of Natural Language Processing in Java Sorcery***

In the mystical world of Java sorcery, we venture into the alluring realm of natural language processing (NLP), where spells decipher the intricacies of human language and grant the power to understand and interact with enchanted texts. In this subchapter, we shall unveil the secrets of NLP in Java, empowering your enchantments to analyze, interpret, and respond to human language in the enchanted realm. With the art of natural language processing in Java sorcery, you can cast spells that bridge the gap between magical beings and the wonders of written words.

Enchantment of NLP with Apache OpenNLP

Prepare to wield the magic of NLP with Apache OpenNLP:

```java
import opennlp.tools.sentdetect.*;
```

```java
import opennlp.tools.tokenize.*;
```

```java
import opennlp.tools.namefind.*;
```

```java
import opennlp.tools.util.*;
```

```java
public class EnchantedOpenNLPSpell {
```

```
    public static void main(String[] args) throws
Exception {



    // Enchanting the world with Apache
OpenNLP...




    // Creating an enchanted sentence detector



    SentenceModel sentenceModel = new
SentenceModel(EnchantedOpenNLPSpell.cl
ass.getResourceAsStream("/models/en-sent.b
in"));



    SentenceDetectorME sentenceDetector =
new SentenceDetectorME(sentenceModel);



    // Creating an enchanted tokenizer
```

```java
        TokenizerModel tokenizerModel = new
TokenizerModel(EnchantedOpenNLPSpell.
class.getResourceAsStream("/models/en-toke
n.bin"));


        TokenizerME tokenizer = new Tokeniz-
erME(tokenizerModel);




        // Enchanting NLP with Apache Open
NLP...




    }



}
```

In this captivating script, we have harnessed the power of Apache OpenNLP for NLP tasks. We create an enchanted sentence detector and tokenizer, allowing you to cast spells that process and analyze the enchanting texts.

<u>The Allure of Natural Language Processing in Java Sorcery</u>

Congratulations, master enchanter! You have now explored the alluring world of natural language processing in Java sorcery. With the power of NLP with Apache OpenNLP, you can craft spells that understand and interact with enchanted texts, unlocking the mysteries of human language and bridging the gap between magical beings and the wonders of written words.

As you continue your journey, prepare to delve deeper into the mysterious frontiers of web development in Java sorcery, the enigmatic art of web security, the captivating world of real-time enchantments, the alluring universe of cloud computing and serverless spells, the enchanting realm of containerization with Docker, the mystical world of distributed systems, the enigmatic universe of data science and machine learning, the captivating journey of big data and analytics, and the captivating world of frontend magic. The alluring world of natural language processing in Java sorcery is but one facet of the vast and ever-enchanting world of Java sorcery that awaits you!

### *Subchapter 18.3: The Enchanted World of Sentiment Analysis in Java Sorcery*

In the mystical world of Java sorcery, we delve into the enchanted realm of sentiment analysis, where spells discern the emotions and sentiments hidden within the enchanted texts. In this subchapter, we shall unveil the secrets of sentiment analysis in Java, empowering your enchantments to understand the feelings and emotions expressed by magical beings in their writings. With the art of sentiment analysis in Java sorcery, you can cast spells that gain deeper insights into the hearts and minds of enchanted entities.

<u>Enchantment of Sentiment Analysis with Stanford NLP</u>

Prepare to wield the magic of sentiment analysis with Stanford NLP:

```java
import edu.stanford.nlp.pipeline.*;
```

```java
import edu.stanford.nlp.sentiment.*;
```

```java
import java.util.*;
```

```java
public class EnchantedStanfordNLP {



public static void main(String[] args) {



    // Enchanting the world with Stanford
NLP...
```

```java
    // Creating an enchanted pipeline


Properties properties = new Properties();


    properties.setProperty("annotators", "to-
kenize,ssplit,pos,parse,sentiment");


    StanfordCoreNLP pipeline = new Stan-
fordCoreNLP(properties);
```

```
        // Enchanting sentiment analysis with
    Stanford NLP...




            }


    }
```

In this captivating script, we have harnessed the power of Stanford NLP for sentiment analysis. We create an enchanted pipeline, allowing you to cast spells that analyze the sentiments and emotions expressed in the enchanted texts.

<u>The Allure of Sentiment Analysis in Java Sorcery</u>

Congratulations, esteemed enchanter! You have now explored the enchanted world of sentiment analysis in Java sorcery. With the power of sentiment analysis with Stanford NLP, you can craft spells that discern the emotions and sentiments hidden within the enchanted texts, gaining deeper insights into the hearts and minds of magical beings.

As you continue your journey, prepare to delve deeper into the mysterious frontiers of web development in Java sorcery, the enigmatic art of web security, the captivating world of real-time enchantments, the alluring universe of cloud computing and serverless spells, the enchanting realm of containerization with Docker, the mystical world of distributed systems, the enigmatic universe of data science and machine learning, the captivating journey of big data and analytics, the alluring world of natural language processing, and the captivating world of frontend magic. The enchanted world of sentiment analysis in Java sorcery is but one facet of the vast and ever-enchanting world of Java sorcery that awaits you!

# CHAPTER NINETEEN

# THE ENIGMATIC ART OF WEB SECURITY IN JAVA SORCERY

Introduction to Web Security in Java Sorcery

Welcome to the enigmatic art of web security in Java sorcery. In this chapter, we shall unveil the secrets of protecting your magical applications from the malevolent forces of the digital realm. With the art of web security in Java sorcery, you can cast spells that fortify your enchanted creations, safeguard sensitive information, and shield them from the clutches of dark enchantments.

The Enchantment of Secure Authentication with Spring Security

Prepare to wield the magic of secure authentication with Spring Security:

```
import org.springframework.security.crypto
.bcrypt.BCryptPasswordEncoder;
```

```java
import org.springframework.security.crypto
.password.PasswordEncoder;



public class EnchantedSpringSecuritySpell {


public static void main(String[] args) {


    // Enchanting the world with Spring
Security...




    // Creating an enchanted password en-
coder


PasswordEncoder passwordEncoder = new
BCryptPasswordEncoder();
```

```java
// Enchanting secure authentication with
Spring Security...



String plainPassword = "abracadabra";



    String encryptedPassword = passwordE
ncoder.encode(plainPassword);



    System.out.println("Encrypted Password:
" + encryptedPassword);



    }


    }
```

In this captivating script, we have harnessed the power of Spring Security for secure authentication. We create an enchanted password encoder, allowing you to cast spells that encrypt and protect user passwords.

<u>The Enchantment of Preventing Cross-Site Scripting (XSS) Attacks</u>

Prepare to weave enchanting spells to prevent Cross-Site Scripting (XSS) attacks:

```java
import org.owasp.encoder.Encode;
```

```java
public class EnchantedXSSProtectionSpell {

public static void main(String[] args) {

    // Enchanting the world with XSS protection...



    // Enchanting XSS protection spells...

    String userInput = "<script>alert('Enchanted XSS Attack!');</script>";

    String protectedInput = Encode.forHtml(userInput);

    System.out.println("Protected Input: " + protectedInput);
```

```
        }



        }
```

In this bewitching script, we have enchanted XSS protection spells using the OWASP Encoder library. You can cast spells that sanitize user inputs and protect your magical applications from malicious scripts.

<u>The Allure of Web Security in Java Sorcery</u>

Congratulations, master enchanter! You have now explored the enigmatic art of web security in Java sorcery. With the power of secure authentication with Spring Security and the enchantment of preventing Cross-Site Scripting (XSS) attacks, you can craft spells that fortify your enchanted creations and shield them from the malevolent forces of the digital realm.

As you continue your journey, prepare to delve deeper into the mysterious frontiers of web development in Java sorcery, the captivating world of real-time enchantments, the alluring universe of cloud computing and serverless spells, the enchanting realm of containerization with Docker, the mystical world of distributed systems, the enigmatic universe of data science and machine learning, the captivating journey of big data and analytics, the alluring world of natural language processing, the enchanted world of sentiment analysis, and the captivating world of frontend magic. The enigmatic art of web security in Java sorcery is but one facet of the vast and ever-enchanting world of Java sorcery that awaits you!

***Subchapter 19.1: The Enchanted World of Cross-Site Request Forgery (CSRF) Protection***

In the mystical world of Java sorcery, we delve into the enchanted realm of Cross-Site Request Forgery (CSRF) protection, where spells shield your magical applications from deceptive and malicious requests. In this subchapter, we shall unveil the secrets of preventing CSRF attacks in Java, empowering your enchantments to detect and thwart unauthorized requests from malevolent entities. With the art of CSRF protection in Java sorcery, you can cast spells that fortify the boundaries of your enchanted realm and guard against dark enchantments seeking to exploit vulnerabilities.

<u>Enchantment of CSRF Protection with Spring Security</u>

Prepare to wield the magic of CSRF protection with Spring Security:

```java
import org.springframework.security.web.csrf.*;
```

```java
public class EnchantedCSRFProtectionSpell
{
```

```java
public static void main(String[] args) {
```

```java
// Enchanting the world with CSRF protection...
```

```
// Creating an enchanted CSRF token
repository


CsrfTokenRepository csrfTokenReposi-
tory = new HttpSessionCsrfTokenReposito-
ry();




// Enchanting CSRF protection with
Spring Security...



    }


    }
```

In this captivating script, we have harnessed the power of Spring Security for CSRF protection. We create an enchanted CSRF token repository, allowing you to cast spells that generate and validate CSRF tokens to defend against CSRF attacks.

The Allure of CSRF Protection in Java Sorcery

Congratulations, esteemed enchanter! You have now explored the enchanted world of Cross-Site Request Forgery (CSRF) protection in Java sorcery. With the power of CSRF protection with Spring Security, you can craft spells that fortify the boundaries of your enchanted realm, guard against dark enchantments, and protect your magical applications from deceptive and malicious requests.

As you continue your journey, prepare to delve deeper into the mysterious frontiers of web development in Java sorcery, the captivating world of real-time enchantments, the alluring universe of cloud computing and serverless spells, the enchanting realm of containerization with Docker, the mystical world of distributed systems, the enigmatic universe of data science and machine learning, the captivating journey of big data and analytics, the alluring world of natural language processing, the enchanted world of sentiment analysis, the enigmatic art of web security, and the captivating world of frontend magic. The enchanted world of Cross-Site Request Forgery (CSRF) protection in Java sorcery is but one facet of the vast and ever-enchanting world of Java sorcery that awaits you!

### *Subchapter 19.2: The Captivating Realm of Role-Based Access Control (RBAC) in Java Sorcery*

In the mystical world of Java sorcery, we venture into the captivating realm of Role-Based Access Control (RBAC), where spells bestow magical entities with precisely defined roles and permissions. In this subchapter, we shall unveil the secrets of implementing RBAC in Java, empowering your enchantments to control access and authorization in the enchanted realm. With the art of RBAC in Java sorcery, you can cast spells that grant the right power to the right beings, ensuring a harmonious and secure magical realm.

<u>Enchantment of RBAC with Spring Security</u>

Prepare to wield the magic of RBAC with Spring Security:

```
import org.springframework.security.core.u
serdetails.*;
```

```
import org.springframework.security.core.a
uthority.SimpleGrantedAuthority;
```

```java
import java.util.*;




public class EnchantedRBACSpell {


    public static void main(String[] args) {


        // Enchanting the world with RBAC...




        // Creating an enchanted user with roles




        List<GrantedAuthority> authorities =
new ArrayList<>();


        authorities.add(new SimpleGrantedAu-
thority("ROLE_WIZARD"));
```

```
        authorities.add(new SimpleGrantedAu-
thority("ROLE_ENCHANTER"));


        UserDetails  enchantedUser  =
new User("wizard123", "abracadabra", au-
thorities);




        // Enchanting RBAC with Spring Secu
rity...



    }



}
```

In this captivating script, we have harnessed the power of Spring Security for RBAC. We create an enchanted user with roles, allowing you to cast spells that grant specific permissions and access based on roles.

<u>The Allure of RBAC in Java Sorcery</u>

Congratulations, master enchanter! You have now delved into the captivating realm of Role-Based Access Control (RBAC) in Java sorcery. With the power of RBAC with Spring Security, you can craft spells that bestow precisely defined roles and permissions upon magical entities, ensuring a harmonious and secure enchanted realm.

As you continue your journey, prepare to delve deeper into the mysterious frontiers of web development in Java sorcery, the alluring universe of cloud computing and serverless spells, the enchanting realm of containerization with Docker, the mystical world of distributed systems, the enigmatic universe of data science and machine learning, the captivating journey of big data and analytics, the alluring world of natural language processing, the enchanted world of sentiment analysis, the enigmatic art of web security, the captivating world of frontend magic, and the captivating realm of Cross-Site Request Forgery (CSRF) protection. The captivating realm of Role-Based Access Control (RBAC) in Java sorcery is but one facet of the vast and ever-enchanting world of Java sorcery that awaits you!

### Subchapter 19.3: The Captivating World of Single Sign-On (SSO) in Java Sorcery

In the mystical world of Java sorcery, we explore the captivating realm of Single Sign-On (SSO), where spells grant magical beings access to multiple enchanted realms with a single authentication. In this subchapter, we shall unveil the secrets of implementing SSO in Java, empowering your enchantments to seamlessly navigate across diverse magical domains. With the art of SSO in Java sorcery, you can cast spells that bestow the power of unified authentication and enchant your users with a seamless and delightful experience.

<u>Enchantment of SSO with Spring Security and OAuth</u>

Prepare to wield the magic of SSO with Spring Security and OAuth:

```
import org.springframework.security.oauth
2.client.*;
```

```
import org.springframework.security.oauth
2.core.*;
```

```
import org.springframework.security.oauth
2.core.user.*;
```

```java
public class EnchantedSSOSpell {

public static void main(String[] args) {

// Enchanting the world with SSO...

    // Creating an enchanted OAuth2 autho-
rized client

    OAuth2AccessToken accessToken =
new OAuth2AccessToken(OAuth2AccessT
oken.TokenType.BEARER, "enchanted_to-
ken", null, null);

    OAuth2User enchantedUser = new
DefaultOAuth2User(null, null, null, "wiz-
ard123", null, accessToken);
```

```
OAuth2AuthorizedClient enchanted-
Client = new OAuth2AuthorizedClient(null,
"enchanted_registration_id", enchantedUser,
accessToken);
```

```
// Enchanting SSO with Spring Security
and OAuth...
```

```
}
```

```
}
```

In this captivating script, we have harnessed the power of Spring Security and OAuth for SSO. We create an enchanted OAuth2 authorized client, allowing you to cast spells that enable seamless navigation across diverse magical domains with a unified authentication.

<u>The Allure of SSO in Java Sorcery</u>

Congratulations, esteemed enchanter! You have now explored the captivating world of Single Sign-On (SSO) in Java sorcery. With the power of SSO with Spring Security and OAuth, you can craft spells that grant magical beings access to multiple enchanted realms with a single authentication, bestowing them with a seamless and delightful experience.

As you continue your journey, prepare to delve deeper into the mysterious frontiers of web development in Java sorcery, the alluring universe of cloud computing and serverless spells, the enchanting realm of containerization with Docker, the mystical world of distributed systems, the enigmatic universe of data science and machine learning, the captivating journey of big data and analytics, the alluring world of natural language processing, the enchanted world of sentiment analysis, the enigmatic art of web security, the captivating world of frontend magic, the captivating realm of Cross-Site Request Forgery (CSRF) protection, and the captivating realm of Role-Based Access Control (RBAC). The captivating world of Single Sign-On (SSO) in Java sorcery is but one facet of the vast and ever-enchanting world of Java sorcery that awaits you!

# CHAPTER TWENTY

# THE CAPTIVATING REALM OF CLOUD COMPUTING AND SERVERLESS SPELLS IN JAVA SORCERY

Introduction to Cloud Computing and Serverless Spells in Java Sorcery

Welcome to the captivating realm of cloud computing and serverless spells in Java sorcery. In this chapter, we shall unveil the secrets of harnessing the power of the cloud to scale your enchantments and cast spells without the burden of managing infrastructure. With the art of cloud computing and serverless spells in Java sorcery, you can craft enchantments that soar to new heights and focus on the magic, leaving the operational complexities to the mystical cloud.

The Enchantment of Cloud Computing with Amazon Web Services (AWS)

Prepare to wield the magic of cloud computing with Amazon Web Services (AWS):

```java
import com.amazonaws.services.s3.*;

import com.amazonaws.services.s3.model.*;

public class EnchantedAWSSpell {

public static void main(String[] args) {

// Enchanting the world with AWS...

// Creating an enchanted AWS S3 client

AmazonS3 enchantedS3Client = Amaz
onS3ClientBuilder.defaultClient();
```

```
        // Enchanting cloud computing with
AWS...




        }




        }
```

In this captivating script, we have harnessed the power of Amazon Web Services (AWS) for cloud computing. We create an enchanted AWS S3 client, allowing you to cast spells that interact with the mystical cloud storage.

The Enchantment of Serverless Spells with AWS Lambda

Prepare to weave enchanting serverless spells with AWS Lambda:

```
import com.amazonaws.services.lambda.A
WSLambda;




import com.amazonaws.services.lambda.A
WSLambdaClientBuilder;




import com.amazonaws.services.lambda.mo
del.InvokeRequest;
```

```java
import com.amazonaws.services.lambda.mo
del.InvokeResult;



public class EnchantedLambdaSpell {


public static void main(String[] args) {



    // Enchanting the world with AWS
Lambda...




    // Creating an enchanted AWS Lambda
client



    AWSLambda enchantedLambdaClient =
AWSLambdaClientBuilder.defaultClient();
```

```
// Enchanting serverless spells with AWS
Lambda...



        }



        }
```

In this bewitching script, we have enchanted serverless spells with AWS Lambda. We create an enchanted AWS Lambda client, allowing you to cast spells that execute code without the need to manage servers.

<u>The Allure of Cloud Computing and Serverless Spells in Java Sorcery</u>

Congratulations, master enchanter! You have now explored the captivating realm of cloud computing and serverless spells in Java sorcery. With the power of cloud computing with Amazon Web Services (AWS) and the enchantment of serverless spells with AWS Lambda, you can craft enchantments that harness the power of the cloud, scale to new heights, and focus on the magic without the burden of managing infrastructure.

As you continue your journey, prepare to delve deeper into the mysterious frontiers of web development in Java sorcery, the alluring universe of containerization with Docker, the mystical world of distributed systems, the enigmatic universe of data science and machine learning, the captivating journey of big data and analytics, the alluring world of natural language processing, the enchanted world of sentiment analysis, the enigmatic art of web security, the captivating world of frontend magic, the captivating realm of Cross-Site Request Forgery (CSRF) protection, the captivating realm of Role-Based Access Control (RBAC), and the captivating world of Single Sign-On (SSO). The captivating realm of cloud computing and serverless spells in Java sorcery is but one facet of the vast and ever-enchanting world of Java sorcery that awaits you!

***Subchapter 20.1: The Enigmatic World of Containerization with Docker in Java Sorcery***

In the mystical world of Java sorcery, we venture into the enigmatic world of containerization with Docker, where spells encapsulate magical applications into portable and isolated containers. In this subchapter, we shall unveil the secrets of containerization in Java, empowering your enchantments to run consistently and reliably across diverse enchanted realms. With the art of containerization with Docker in Java sorcery, you can cast spells that weave enchantments into self-contained and transportable entities.

Enchantment of Containerization with Docker

Prepare to wield the magic of containerization with Docker:

```java
import com.github.dockerjava.api.*;



import com.github.dockerjava.core.*;



import com.github.dockerjava.api.model.*;




public class EnchantedDockerSpell {


public static void main(String[] args) {


// Enchanting the world with Docker...
```

```java
// Creating an enchanted Docker client


DockerClient enchantedDockerClient =
DockerClientBuilder.getInstance().build();




// Enchanting containerization with
Docker...



}



}
```

In this captivating script, we have harnessed the power of Docker for containerization. We create an enchanted Docker client, allowing you to cast spells that interact with the mystical containers.

<u>The Allure of Containerization with Docker in Java Sorcery</u>

Congratulations, esteemed enchanter! You have now delved into the enigmatic world of containerization with Docker in Java sorcery. With the power of containerization with Docker, you can craft spells that encapsulate your magical applications into portable and isolated containers, ensuring consistency and reliability across diverse enchanted realms.

As you continue your journey, prepare to delve deeper into the mysterious frontiers of web development in Java sorcery, the mystical world of distributed systems, the enigmatic universe of data science and machine learning, the captivating journey of big data and analytics, the alluring world of natural language processing, the enchanted world of sentiment analysis, the enigmatic art of web security, the captivating world of frontend magic, the captivating realm of Cross-Site Request Forgery (CSRF) protection, the captivating realm of Role-Based Access Control (RBAC), the captivating world of Single Sign-On (SSO), the captivating realm of cloud computing and serverless spells, and the captivating world of web security. The enigmatic world of containerization with Docker in Java sorcery is but one facet of the vast and ever-enchanting world of Java sorcery that awaits you!

### *Subchapter 20.2: The Mystical World of Distributed Systems in Java Sorcery*

In the mystical world of Java sorcery, we delve into the enchanting realm of distributed systems, where spells orchestrate the collaboration of magical entities to achieve unparalleled feats of performance and scalability. In this subchapter, we shall unveil the secrets of building distributed systems in Java, empowering your enchantments to communicate and coordinate across diverse magical beings. With the art of distributed systems in Java sorcery, you can cast spells that unleash the full potential of collaborative enchantments.

<u>Enchantment of Distributed Communication with Apache Kafka</u>

Prepare to wield the magic of distributed communication with Apache Kafka:

```
import org.apache.kafka.clients.producer.*;
```

```
import org.apache.kafka.clients.consumer.*;
```

```
import org.apache.kafka.common.serializati
on.*;
```

```java
public class EnchantedKafkaSpell {

public static void main(String[] args) {

    // Enchanting the world with Apache
Kafka...




// Creating an enchanted Kafka producer


    Properties producerProps = new Proper-
ties();


    producerProps.put(ProducerConfig.B
OOTSTRAP_SERVERS_CONFIG, "local-
host:9092");
```

```
    producerProps.put(ProducerConfig.KE
Y_SERIALIZER_CLASS_CONFIG, Strin
gSerializer.class.getName());


    producerProps.put(ProducerConfig.VA
LUE_SERIALIZER_CLASS_CONFIG, S
tringSerializer.class.getName());


    KafkaProducer<String, String> enchant-
edProducer = new KafkaProducer<>(pro-
ducerProps);




// Creating an enchanted Kafka consumer


    Properties consumerProps = new Prop-
erties();


consumerProps.put(ConsumerConfig.B
OOTSTRAP_SERVERS_CONFIG, "local-
host:9092");
```

```java
consumerProps.put(ConsumerConfig.KEY_
DESERIALIZER_CLASS_CONFIG,
StringDeserializer.class.getName());


consumerProps.put(ConsumerConfig.VAL
UE_DESERIALIZER_CLASS_CONFIG,
StringDeserializer.class.getName());


consumerProps.put(ConsumerConfig.G
ROUP_ID_CONFIG, "enchanted-group");


KafkaConsumer<String, String> enchant-
edConsumer = new KafkaConsumer<>(con-
sumerProps);


// Enchanting distributed communication
with Apache Kafka...


}
```

}

In this captivating script, we have harnessed the power of Apache Kafka for distributed communication. We create an enchanted Kafka producer and consumer, allowing you to cast spells that communicate and coordinate across magical beings.

<u>The Allure of Distributed Systems in Java Sorcery</u>

Congratulations, master enchanter! You have now explored the mystical world of distributed systems in Java sorcery. With the power of distributed communication with Apache Kafka, you can craft spells that orchestrate the collaboration of magical entities, achieving unparalleled feats of performance and scalability.

As you continue your journey, prepare to delve deeper into the mysterious frontiers of web development in Java sorcery, the enigmatic universe of data science and machine learning, the captivating journey of big data and analytics, the alluring world of natural language processing, the enchanted world of sentiment analysis, the enigmatic art of web security, the captivating world of frontend magic, the captivating realm of Cross-Site Request Forgery (CSRF) protection, the captivating realm of Role-Based Access Control (RBAC), the captivating world of Single Sign-On (SSO), the captivating realm of cloud computing and serverless spells, the captivating world of web security, and the enigmatic world of containerization with Docker. The mystical world of distributed systems in Java sorcery is but one facet of the vast and ever-enchanting world of Java sorcery that awaits you!

**Subchapter 20.3: The Enigmatic Universe of Data Science and Machine Learning in Java Sorcery**

In the mystical world of Java sorcery, we venture into the enigmatic universe of data science and machine learning, where spells uncover hidden patterns and insights from vast amounts of enchanted data. In this subchapter, we shall unveil the secrets of data science and machine learning in Java, empowering your enchantments to predict, classify, and analyze the magical wonders that lie within the data realm. With the art of data science and machine learning in Java sorcery, you can cast spells that unlock the full potential of enchanted data and gain unparalleled understanding of the enchanted world.

<u>Enchantment of Machine Learning with Weka</u>

Prepare to wield the magic of machine learning with Weka:

```java
import weka.core.*;

import weka.classifiers.trees.J48;

public class EnchantedWekaSpell {

public static void main(String[] args) throws
Exception {

// Enchanting the world with Weka...

// Creating an enchanted dataset

Instances enchantedDataset = ... // Load
or create your enchanted dataset
```

```
    // Creating an enchanted J48 decision tree
classifier


J48 enchantedClassifier = new J48();



    enchantedClassifier.buildClassifier(ench
antedDataset);




    // Enchanting machine learning with
Weka...



    }



    }
```

In this captivating script, we have harnessed the power of Weka for machine learning. We create an enchanted dataset and a decision tree classifier, allowing you to cast spells that train and apply machine learning models on magical data.

The Allure of Data Science and Machine Learning in Java Sorcery

Congratulations, esteemed enchanter! You have now delved into the enigmatic universe of data science and machine learning in Java sorcery. With the power of machine learning with Weka, you can craft spells that uncover hidden patterns and insights from enchanted data, predict and classify enchanted phenomena, and gain unparalleled understanding of the enchanted world.

As you continue your journey, prepare to delve deeper into the mysterious frontiers of web development in Java sorcery, the captivating journey of big data and analytics, the alluring world of natural language processing, the enchanted world of sentiment analysis, the enigmatic art of web security, the captivating world of frontend magic, the captivating realm of Cross-Site Request Forgery (CSRF) protection, the captivating realm of Role-Based Access Control (RBAC), the captivating world of Single Sign-On (SSO), the captivating realm of cloud computing and serverless spells, the captivating world of web security, the enigmatic world of containerization with Docker, and the mystical world of distributed systems. The enigmatic universe of data science and machine learning in Java sorcery is but one facet of the vast and ever-enchanting world of Java sorcery that awaits you!

# CONCLUSION: EMBARKING ON AN EVER-ENCHANTING JOURNEY IN JAVA SORCERY

**Conclusion: Embarking on an Ever-Enchanting Journey in Java Sorcery**

Dear fellow enchanter,

As we draw near to the end of our captivating journey through the mystical world of Java sorcery, we find ourselves in awe of the boundless enchantments that this realm has to offer. From the arcane mysteries of web development to the alluring universe of cloud computing, from the enigmatic art of web security to the captivating wonders of data science and machine learning, we have explored a vast and ever-enchanting tapestry of knowledge and magic.

Through the pages of this enchanted book, we have delved into the heart of Java sorcery, casting spells with code, unleashing the power of libraries and frameworks, and creating magical applications that weave enchantments in the digital realm. We have learned to wield the magic of Java to create web applications that dance harmoniously with the mystical internet, building frontend spells that enchant users and backend conjurations that wield the forces of data and logic.

With every chapter, we have discovered new dimensions of magic: the enigmatic world of web security, where spells shield our creations from malevolent forces; the captivating realm of cloud computing and serverless spells, where we harness the power of the mystical cloud; the mystical art of distributed systems, where we orchestrate the collaboration of magical beings; and the profound wonders of data science and machine learning, where we unlock the secrets hidden within vast amounts of enchanted data.

Our journey has been filled with the allure of natural language processing, the enchanting world of sentiment analysis, the captivating realm of Cross-Site Request Forgery (CSRF) protection, and the captivating realm of Role-Based Access Control (RBAC). We have explored the captivating world of Single Sign-On (SSO), the enigmatic world of containerization with Docker, and the captivating world of frontend magic.

Yet, as every journey in Java sorcery knows no end, we realize that there are always new enchantments to master, new realms to explore, and new wonders to uncover. As you continue your voyage as an esteemed enchanter, remember that the world of Java sorcery is ever-evolving and ever-enchanting, with new libraries, frameworks, and spells awaiting your discovery.

May your enchantments continue to flourish and may you wield the power of Java sorcery with wisdom and creativity. Let your spells be a force of enchantment and good in the digital realm, bringing joy and wonder to all who encounter them.

Farewell, fellow enchanter, and may your journey through the mystical world of Java sorcery be an ever-enchanting one!

Yours in magic,

Master Enchanter of Java Sorcery